Science 5

for Christian Schools®

"Thus saith the Lord the maker thereof, the Lord that formed it, to establish it; the Lord is his name; Call unto me, and I will answer thee, and shew thee great and mighty things, which thou knowest not."
Jeremiah 33:2-3

Dawn L. Watkins

Consultants

Joseph Hensen, Ph.D.
Chairman, Division of Natural Science, Bob Jones University

Albert Isaak, Ph.D.
Professor, Department of Biology, Bob Jones University

Margene Ranieri, Ph.D.
Professor, Department of Biology, Bob Jones University

Linda Hayner, Ph.D.
Professor, Department of Social Studies, Bob Jones University

Special acknowledgment is given to Candace Jamison for organizing the scope and sequence of the project.

NOTE:
The fact that materials produced by other publishers are referred to in this volume does not constitute an endorsement by Bob Jones University Press of the content or theological position of these materials or any other materials produced by such publishers. The position of Bob Jones University Press, and the University itself, is well known. Any references and ancillary materials are listed as an aid to the student or the teacher in an attempt to maintain accepted academic standards of the publishing industry.

SCIENCE 5 for Christian Schools®
Second Edition

Dawn L. Watkins

Produced in cooperation with the Bob Jones University Department of Science Education of the School of Education, the College of Arts and Science, and Bob Jones Elementary School

ISBN 0-89084-435-6

20 19 18 17 16 15 14 13 12 11 10 9 8

Contents

 # The Study of Fossils

"Behold now behemoth, which I made."

Job 40:15

If you had a time machine that could take you anywhere, where would you go? Imagine that you have such equipment and that you set it for the time of the dinosaurs. You arrive there with your camera and your notebook and begin to record everything you see and hear. What you would be doing is observing.

Science is the collection of facts gained by observing. All scientists use their senses to get information. They record information and try to interpret it. The information is fact, but the interpretations are opinion. The ideas that scientists come up with by studying the facts are *theories*. If a theory is tested and retested and produces the same results, then a theory may become a fact.

How can the study of something like dinosaurs be scientific? No one alive has ever observed a dinosaur. And there are no time machines. We know dinosaurs by their bones, you say. And you are right. The study of fossils, honestly and carefully done, can tell us much about these giant beasts. *Fossil* comes from a Latin word meaning "something dug up." How else might scientists discover fossils besides digging them up? Sometimes fossils are exposed when the rocks they are in become weathered. The rocks wear away, and the bones in them appear. What we observe about the bones is fact; what are the assumptions we make about the animals to which they belonged?

2

The Bible may be referring to a dinosaur in Job 40:15-24. The behemoth mentioned there is a large, powerful beast that eats plants. It has a tail like a cedar tree, and its bones are as strong as brass and iron. It lives in a swampy place, drinking great quantities of water. This description could fit a dinosaur such as the Diplodocus. Apart from this passage in Job, however, there is no written record of dinosaurs. Anything we learn about these giants must come from fossils.

Early Discoveries

Fossils are not a modern discovery. They have been found decorating axe heads and necklaces of thousands of years ago. The ancient Greeks collected fossils and also studied them. Around 450 B.C. Herodotus wrote a book about seashell fossils that he had found far inland. He even ventured to say that they had been left there as the sea withdrew. The Chinese were collecting what they called ''stone swallows'' in the fourth century. Today we know stone swallows are a kind of fossil shellfish. Fossils were so popular in China that people made and sold imitations.

A scientist in England in the 1600s wrote a book describing and illustrating his fossil finds. Robert Plot was probably the first person to actually describe a dinosaur bone. He was also the first since Herodotus to believe that the fossils had once been living creatures. Most other people thought that fossils were special kinds of stone.

A little later, the French scientist Baron Georges Cuvier studied only fossils with backbones for over forty years. He published all his observations. His work was the beginning of modern *paleontology,* the study of ancient living things.

In the early 1800s in England, a Mrs. Mantell discovered some huge animal teeth in broken rocks. Her husband, Dr. Mantell, had never seen anything quite like them, and so he sent them to some other scientists. They said that the teeth belonged to a rhinoceros. But Dr. Mantell did not think so. He went back to where his wife had found the teeth and did some more digging. He discovered many more fossil bones, enough to make him believe that the animal had been some kind of giant lizard.

Sir Richard Owen, another British scientist, studied the fossils and also the skeletons of modern animals. He found differences between lizards he was familiar with and the giant "lizards" of fossil record. He decided that the animals the fossils revealed should be classified as a separate group. In 1841, he told the British Association for the Advancement of Science that he had chosen the name *dinosauria*. *Deinos* means "terrible" and *sauros* means "lizard" in Greek. What do you think Owen wanted to indicate about the animals in that group?

Fossil Evidence

Fossils form when living things are suddenly buried. Why would the burial have to be immediate? If plants and animals are not covered right away, they decompose or are eaten. Also, the deeper they are buried, the more likely they are to become fossils. Why do you think that is true? The less air that can get to a buried plant or animal, the better it is protected from bacteria. The best fossils are made when the sudden, deep burial happens underwater. Most fossils appear to have been formed by being buried under water. Water slows decay by keeping air out.

Animals and plants buried suddenly and deeply may change chemically. Minerals from the water or sediment may fill in the pores of the bone or shell. The bone's original shape stays the same, but the fossil is usually heavier than the original organism. Why do you think this is so?

There are other kinds of fossil records, though. Sometimes a buried organism dissolves without being filled with minerals. Then it leaves a space in the rock in a perfect outline of itself. The space is called a *mold*. If the mold later fills in with sediment, a *cast* forms. Footprints are preserved in casts. If you find a fossil mold, you can make your own cast from it. Why do you think scientists make casts from molds? Casts let us see what the original looked like better than the molds do.

Molds of extremely thin things, such as leaves, are called *imprints*. Another kind of fossil is formed when plants decay and leave a black outline in rock. The outline forms when parts of the plant turn to carbon, an element found in all living things. The fossils made this way are just thin layers of carbon bonded to the rock.

INSIDE Information

Sometimes whole animals or plants become fossils. Explorers in Siberia were shocked to find the perfectly preserved bodies of wooly mammoths in the frozen soil. The mammoths' coats were in good condition and the meat on these fossils was so well kept that the explorers fed their dogs with it. Many whole fossils have been pulled from tar pits as well.

Finding Out . . .

About Molds and Casts

1. Get some modeling clay, a Styrofoam bowl, some shells or fossils, plaster of Paris, water, a wooden spoon, some petroleum jelly or cooking spray, a few paper towels, and a pair of tweezers.

2. Put the modeling clay into the bowl. Make sure that the clay is at least an inch deep and fairly smooth. Put petroleum jelly or cooking spray around the container sides above the clay. Put jelly or spray lightly on the shell or fossil. Press the fossil or shell into the clay and then carefully remove it. You may have to use the tweezers. Repeat to make another mold, if you like. Do not crowd the molds too close together.

3. Mix the plaster until it is about the consistency of pancake batter. Cover the molds with plaster of Paris. Let the plaster dry. When the plaster is hard, tear the sides of the bowl away. Use the bottom of the bowl to help peel the clay off the plaster cast.

4. How does the mold compare with the cast?

Finding Out . . .

About Carbon Outlines

1. Get a piece of cardboard (such as in a box of typing paper), a candle, some petroleum jelly, a leaf or fern frond, paper towels, two sheets of smooth white paper, tweezers, and matches.

2. As your teacher instructs you, coat the cardboard with a thin layer of petroleum jelly and smoke it with the candle. Do not do this part by yourself!

3. Carefully lay the leaf or frond vein-side down on the blackened cardboard. Without moving the leaf, put a piece of paper over the leaf and rub it firmly several times. Lift the paper and gently pull the leaf out of the jelly.

4. Lay the leaf vein-side down on a clean piece of paper. Again without moving the leaf, put a sheet of paper over it and rub firmly several times. Lift the paper and carefully pull up the leaf.

5. Look at the carbon outline. Is this a fossil? Why do you think the imprints on rocks are different? Where do you think the carbon comes from in fossil outlines?

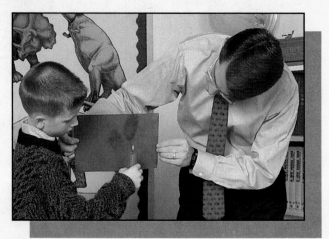

Finding fossils is one thing; interpreting them is another. We can learn many things from fossil records. But fossils cannot tell us everything. Sometimes, if the fossil is complete or almost complete, we can tell what the animal or plant looked like, what its structure was like. We can also learn about the organism's size. What things cannot be learned from fossil remains? Can we know what color the animal was? Can we tell whether it was warm-blooded or cold-blooded? Sometimes bits of skin or a feather are fossilized. But even then no one can be sure that other animals had the same appearance as these discoveries indicate.

Sometimes fossil finds give us clues about the animal's habits. If a fossilized shark has shrimp in its stomach, we can assume it ate shrimp. If a fossil has wings, we think it probably flew. Can you think of a modern creature with wings that does not fly? What can you say about drawing conclusions about an animal's behavior from its fossil?

Fossils can also let us know something about the animal's environment. For example, if we know that shrimp live in warm water and if we find a shark fossil with shrimp in its stomach, what conclusion can we make about the shark? We can say it lived in warm water. But can we say that it also lived in cold water? No, we cannot. What might be a clue to its having lived in cold water?

Many times fossils indicate how the animals died. Often insects are found encased in amber. Amber is fossilized resin, a sticky substance produced by plants. What do you think killed the insects? They probably got stuck in the resin and starved. What else might have happened? They might have been smothered in more resin. Dozens of woolly mammoths were frozen, their last meal still in their stomachs. How do we know that these animals died suddenly? However, no one really knows why the Siberian mammoths died. What else might we learn from studying these fossils?

Most fossils indicate that the animals died in a great *catastrophe,* a sudden, violent change in the earth's surface. Dinosaur bones are found in jumbled, twisted heaps. Land and sea creatures are discovered buried together, some flattened thinner than this book by the crush of sediment above them. Almost all fossils seem to have been formed when animals drowned and were immediately covered by sand and soil. Furthermore, fossils are found all over the world–in deserts, on mountains, in caves, or under water.

Scientists interpret these clues in different ways. Some scientists think that the evidence shows a slow, slow burying. They believe that animals and plants got swept downstream and trapped. After a while the bones were covered with sediment and after thousands or millions of years fossils formed. However, this theory cannot explain fossils that are found standing vertically in several layers of sediment. What would keep the top of the fossil from rotting during the great amount of time needed for the next sediment layers to form? It would be rare conditions indeed that would preserve a plant or animal in the open air for centuries.

Transporting and Rebuilding Fossils

Part of the difficulty in interpreting fossils is how they have to be taken from the earth and carried elsewhere. Several techniques were invented in the 1870s during the American ''fossil rush.'' Dinosaur bones, like gold, were in great demand. Men set out to dig for the fossil treasures, competing to bring back the best or the most skeletons.

Then, as now, the fossils first have to be uncovered. Sometimes brushes are enough to sweep away sediment and expose the find. At other times paleontologists need small hammers and chisels. When the fossil can be clearly seen, the paleontologist makes and labels a map of the entire specimen. Why do you think he draws a picture of it before it is out of the ground? Later, when the bones are taken to a museum or a science center, the map helps workers put the skeleton together. The paleontologist paints a number on each bone and records the number on his map. He also paints along any cracks in the bones so that if any break later he can put them back together correctly.

Once the bones are carefully mapped, they are removed from the ground. Usually, sections of the surrounding rock and dirt are taken with the bones. If a bone is really large, it may have to be freed entirely so that it can be lifted and transported. A hundred years ago, men used dynamite and picks to get the bones out. Today, the searchers have electric drills and different explosives, but the work is still long and hard.

Next, the fossils have to be packed and carried from the digging site to where they can be studied. In 1870 one adventurer, E. D. Cope, found–as many others had–that even the most carefully packed bones broke all to pieces on the rough wagon ride back to the East. He was determined to find a way to protect his hard-gotten fossils. One day as he was eating rice, he had an idea. He asked the cook to boil the rice into a paste. Then Cope dipped strips of burlap in the paste and wrapped a bone with the strips. The paste dried hard, protecting the bone. Soon everyone was using Cope's method, and many more specimens began arriving safely.

Later, paleontologists began using plaster of Paris and canvas strips. They learned to wrap the bones in wet paper first so that the plaster would not stick to the fossils and damage them. Today they wrap the bones in aluminum foil and then cover them with a plastic foam. But the basic method is the one Cope used in the 1800s. Even today the trip from the site to the museum may be rough and difficult. Most searchers build wooden crates on the site to fit the bones they are taking out of the ground.

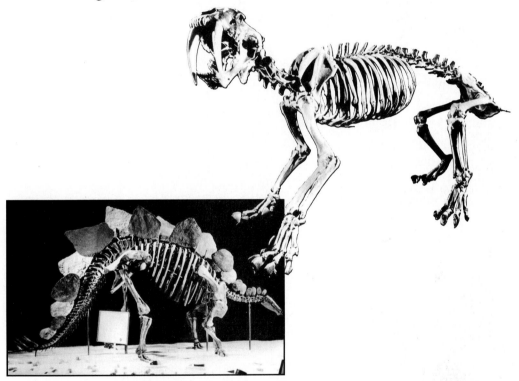

Once the bones arrive at a museum or science center, they have to be cleaned and assembled. Some bones can be washed clean in water. Some have to be chiseled out of the stone they are encased in. Occasionally, technicians use acids to clean the fossils. When the bones are completely stripped, they are ready to be studied and reassembled.

Paleozoology

Have you ever seen a skeleton of a dinosaur in a museum? It was probably put together by a special kind of paleontologist. Scientists who study the fossil remains of animals with backbones are called *paleozoologists. Paleo* comes from a word meaning "long ago." *Zoology* is the study of animals. To do their jobs, paleozoologists need to know many sciences.

By learning how present-day animals look and move, paleozoologists can sometimes discover how extinct animals lived. For example, an animal's teeth can often tell the scientist whether the animal was a meat-eater or a plant-eater. Meat-eating animals usually have short incisor teeth in front, long canine teeth on the sides, and molars in the back for crushing. When a paleozoologist finds a skull with canine teeth, he guesses that the animal was a meat-eater. Plant-eaters generally have flat grinding teeth in back. They may have incisors for nipping like the meat-eaters. There is usually a space between the front and the back teeth.

The scientist can use the skeletons of animals that exist today to help him arrange fossil bones into skeletons. Most vertebrates–animals with backbones–have similarities in their skeleton structure. Can you think of any problems that might come from using modern animals to reconstruct extinct ones? What are scientists who use this method assuming? They believe that all vertebrates have always had basically the same structure.

Besides animal anatomy, a paleozoologist needs to know about soil and rocks, chemistry, plants, and basic engineering. He even has to be something of an artist, forming bones and sculpting lifelike models from skeletons. Most paleozoologists work for science centers or natural history museums. They are the ones who usually respond when someone calls in to say he has found a dinosaur bone in his yard.

Sometimes fossil skeletons are found complete. These skeletons are important because no one has to guess about the arrangement of the bones. Most skeletons, however, are incomplete. Bones are found scattered and broken, usually across wide areas. Often the bones of many animals are mixed together. Most of the time, several bones are missing altogether. Such finds present several problems for scientists. Suppose you came upon a pile of bones. You had no idea what animal they were from or even if they were from the same animal. How would you go about making a skeleton from the bones?

Scientists have few clues to help them. Frequently they can go by what they know of animals living today. Also they can sometimes find some information in the rocks where the bones were found. Either way paleontologists have to make guesses. From time to time, complete skeletons turn up that show guesses to be wrong. Probably the best-known dinosaur for many years, the Brontosaurus, is now known to be a combination of the body of a Diplodocus and the skull of an Apatosaurus. The skull had been found several miles from the rest of the bones. When skeletons of the Diplodocus and the Apatosaurus came to light, the Brontosaurus became a mythical animal.

A paleontologist will often look at the rock the fossil was found in. If he finds plant remains in the rock with a plant-eating animal's skeleton, he may conclude that the animal ate those plants. What must he assume if he concludes that? He believes the animal died where it ate its last meal. Does this have to be so?

When parts of a skeleton are missing, scientists make artificial replacements. When do you think this method works best? It works best when most of the animal's real bones are found. It becomes unscientific when most of the skeleton is manmade. In the drawing on this page, the colored portions show the real bones. The rest of the skeleton is a paleontologist's idea of what the animal looked like. When you see a skeleton in a museum, always check to see how much of it is real and how much is reconstructed.

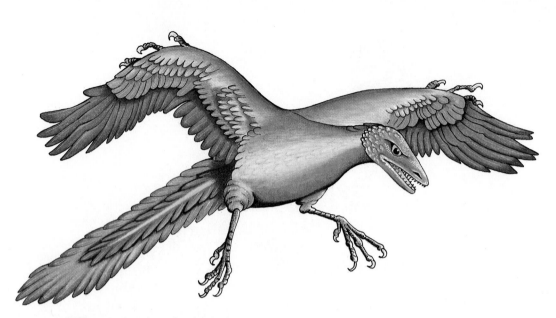

When scientists look at the many skeletons, both complete and reconstructed, they try to put the dinosaurs into groups. The ones that look alike are put into groups. Some scientists think the similarities between certain groups show how animals evolved from one kind to another. For example, some theorize that the Archaeopteryx shows one step reptiles took toward becoming birds.

The Bible, however, says that animals bring forth "after their kind." That is, parent animals will produce young like themselves. Scientists who accept the Bible read the fossil record differently. They see the Archaeopteryx as a kind of bird that is now extinct, not as a link in a chain of changes.

"These are the generations of the heavens and of the earth when they were created, in the day that the Lord God made the earth and the heavens, And every plant of the field before it was in the earth, and every herb of the field before it grew: for the Lord God had not caused it to rain upon the earth, and there was not a man to till the ground. But there went up a mist from the earth, and watered the whole face of the ground."

Genesis 2:4-6

The End of an Era

Since dinosaur bones are found worldwide and in great numbers, we know that at one time the earth held many "terrible lizards." What, then, happened to them? Why are there no dinosaurs today?

The fossils of plants seem to tell us that when the dinosaurs were plentiful, the earth was bringing forth huge plants in abundance. Most scientists believe that the climate all over the earth was at one time like it is now in places such as Hawaii. That kind of climate could produce the plants necessary to feed the plant-eating dinosaurs.

Since the climate of the earth now has extremes in temperatures and the plants are not as large or as plentiful, something must have happened to change the conditions. Some scientists think that the earth was bombarded by meteors. Others think that a star came too close to the earth and disrupted the atmosphere. No one knows for sure. Many people who believe the Bible think that the Flood recorded in Genesis may have changed the earth and its atmosphere.

Rain happens because water vapor in the air comes together and falls to earth. Before the Flood, there was no rain. The earth was like a giant terrarium, being kept moist by dew and the water-heavy air around it. During the Flood, God caused the water in the atmosphere to condense and fall as rain. At the same time, all the great fountains of the deep opened, and water spewed forth from inside the earth as well. The tumult that followed would be enough to change the earth forever.

After the rains of the Flood stopped, the atmosphere–now holding far less water–would not give the same covering to the earth. Temperatures would begin to vary more, plants that needed the old climate could not grow, and shortly, the animals that ate those plants would begin to die off. The dinosaurs, needing such tremendous amounts of food, would not be able to survive in the new conditions.

Since no one can prove what happened, what you believe about such things is a matter of faith. Those who do not believe the Bible put their faith in the guesses paleontologists and other scientists make. Everyone has to decide for himself which explanation best fits the facts.

"And God remembered Noah, and every living thing, and all the cattle that was with him in the ark: and God made a wind to pass over the earth, and the waters asswaged; The fountains also of the deep and the windows of heaven were stopped, and the rain from heaven was restrained; And the waters returned from off the earth continually: and after the end of the hundred and fifty days the waters were abated."

Genesis 8:1-3

 # Oceans

"The sea is his, and he made it."   *Psalm 95:5*

From a spaceship, the earth looks like a blue jewel on black velvet. The earth looks blue because it is covered mostly with water. In fact, if the planet surface were divided into ten parts, seven of them would be water, and only three would be land. If you look at a globe, you can see that the earth's surface looks like a giant body of water interrupted occasionally by landmasses.

The largest, deepest ocean in the world is the Pacific. All the landmasses of earth would fit into it. It stretches from South America to Alaska and from western North America to Australia. The Arctic Ocean, the shallowest and the coldest, lies around the North Pole. The Atlantic and the Indian are two other oceans. What do you think all the oceans have in common?

Ocean Water

Perhaps you have heard the fable about the salt mill that kept spilling salt into the ocean until the whole ocean became salty. For as long as men have gone to sea, they have been making up tales about its saltiness. Why do you think that the oceans are salty?

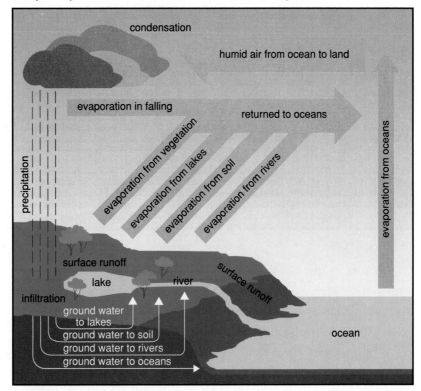

Saltiness

All the water on the earth is part of a great *hydrological cycle*. *Hydro* refers to "water" and *logia* means a "study." Scientists who study water are *hydrologists*. All the water on earth goes through a cycle of being taken up into the atmosphere and released as rain or snow. Then it becomes part of rivers or lakes or seas again, until it is drawn again into the atmosphere. Part of this cycle accounts for the saltiness of seawater.

The rivers of the land run into the oceans. As they do, they carry minerals from the land with them. As the river water mixes with the ocean water, the minerals from the land become part of the ocean. When the sun and wind lift moisture from the ocean surface, the minerals are left behind. When the water returns to the earth as rain, it once again becomes part of rivers that run to the sea, carrying more minerals. Why do you think that seas in warm climates are saltier than those in cold climates?

Rain also falls in the oceans, adding fresh water as regularly as the rivers add minerals. And recently, freshwater springs have been found under the sea. Perhaps it is these springs referred to in Job 38:16—"Hast thou entered into the springs of the sea?"

"All the rivers run into the sea; yet the sea is not full."

Ecclesiastes 1:7

Movement

Water in the ocean is always moving. The tides rise and fall, as the water is pulled by the moon and pushed by the earth's spin. The tide rises twice a day, but ocean water moves in other ways as well.

Perhaps you have been to a beach and seen the waves rippling across the surface of the ocean as far as you could see. And perhaps you saw a ball or a bird bobbing on the water not too far from shore. If you waited for the ball or the bird to come closer to shore on the waves, you probably got tired of waiting.

Waves do not move water forward, but rather up and down. The only time water actually moves forward with a wave is when there is a strong wind or when the wave breaks against the shore. Drops of water making up waves travel in rough circles, moving up and slightly forward and then down and back. Most of the steady action of ocean waves is caused by wind.

Storm winds can cause dangerous high waves that batter the coasts. Waves in storms can be thirty feet high or higher. In 1933 some sailors in the Pacific Ocean saw a wave 112 feet high, higher than a ten-story building.

The most dangerous waves are *tsunamis,* commonly known as tidal waves. They are caused not by wind but by sudden earthquakes or volcanoes under the ocean. These huge waves sometimes surge across the ocean at more then 500 miles an hour. When they near the shore, the killer waves can be 200 feet high. They can level everything in their path, even destroy whole towns. In the 1880s, 36,000 people died when a tsunami smashed over the island of Java. Today, with telephones and radios nearly everywhere, people usually have enough warning to get away from an approaching tsunami.

Ocean Currents

Labels on maps: Pacific/Alaska, Gulf Stream, North Equatorial, Equatorial Counter, South Equatorial, Peru, West Wind Drift, Falkland, Gulf Stream, North Equatorial, Equatorial Counter, Brazil, West Wind Drift, Greenland, W. Greenland, E. Greenland, Norwegian, North Atlantic Drift, North Equatorial, Canary, South Equatorial

Many seafarers learned early that certain places in the oceans made travel swifter and some places slowed ships down. Benjamin Franklin noticed that American ships could travel to England faster than they could travel back to America. With the help of his sea captain cousin, Franklin identified a *current,* a steady flow of water, in the Atlantic Ocean. We call it the Gulf Stream.

A few years later, an officer in the United States Navy, Matthew Maury, was reading Psalm 8. When he read the phrase ''paths of the sea'' there, he began to wonder what it meant. He believed that if the Bible said there are paths in the sea that, then, there are paths in the sea. He started to collect all the information he could from sea captains and from his own experience and to study it. What he found after years of work changed travel on the seas forever. He found that the seas do indeed have ''paths'' in them, streams of steadily moving water. His maps of the currents helped ships make faster, smoother journeys all over the world. Lt. Maury became known as ''The Pathfinder of the

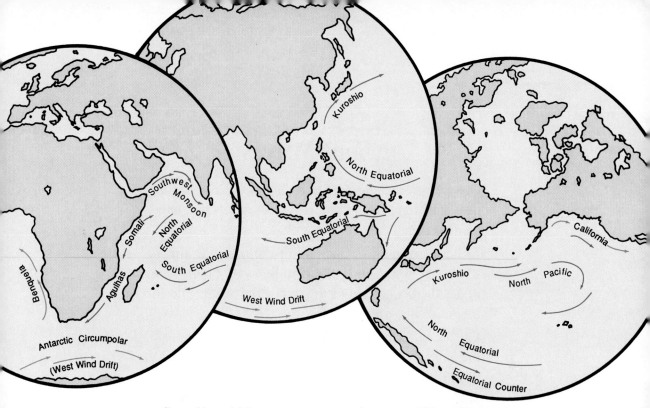

Seas,'' and his name appears on every Pilot Chart printed by the United States Government.

Forty important currents flow constantly through the oceans. Together they make five great loops, or *gyres,* that circle through the seas. Look at the map of the currents. Which ones would you take to get from New York to Norway?

No one knows what makes the currents move the way they do. Possibly it is the combination of the earth's rotation, the heating of the sun, the shape of the oceans, and the winds. Christians can see God's care and design in the currents. These regular, immense streams of water carry heat away from the equator and bring cold from the polar regions toward the equator, making the climate of the whole earth milder.

Currents also carry food for the animals that live in the sea. And they carry plants and animals to other locations. It is possible, for example, that a ripe coconut dropped into the sea may float to a distant shore, sprout, and become a tree.

Finding Out . . .

About Waves

1. Get a large rectangular cake pan, two blocks of wood nearly as long as the pan is wide, some sand, and some water.

2. Build a "beach" at one end of the pan with the sand, slanting it up to the rim. Put a block of wood under the beach end of the pan. Pour water into the pan until the water touches the edge of the "beach."

3. Put the other block in the water at the end opposite the sand. Slowly move the block forward toward the sand. Stop about halfway across the pan. Wait a few seconds and repeat. Repeat at least fifteen times. What happens to the beach? Why?

About the Ocean Floor

1. Get the model of the ocean from your teacher, a ruler, the chart from your notebook, and a pencil.

2. Work with a partner. Put your ruler into the water at one end of the model. Let it go down until it hits bottom. How deep is the water? Record the measurement on the chart. Move the ruler forward two inches and measure the depth of the water. Record the measurement. Continue measuring at two-inch intervals to the other side of the model.

3. Draw a line connecting the marks on your chart. What have you made? What conclusions can you draw from your chart? What can you guess about the floor of the model?

Landscape of the Oceans

Imagine that you could breathe underwater without special equipment and that you could walk underwater as easily as you walk in a park. Then suppose that you were going to take a walking tour of the oceans. You would see sights more spectacular than you have ever seen on land.

As you walk out into the surf, you go down a slowly sloping rock platform called a *continental shelf.* These ledges, covered with sand or gravel or rocks, rim the continents. Beyond the shelf, you would find yourself running down a sudden drop-off called the *continental slope.* You may have to cross one of the deeply eroded valleys called *submarine canyons.* Some are as large as the Grand Canyon. Today scientists observe nothing happening there that could erode such canyons. Many scientists who are Christians believe that canyons were carved out after the Flood, as water

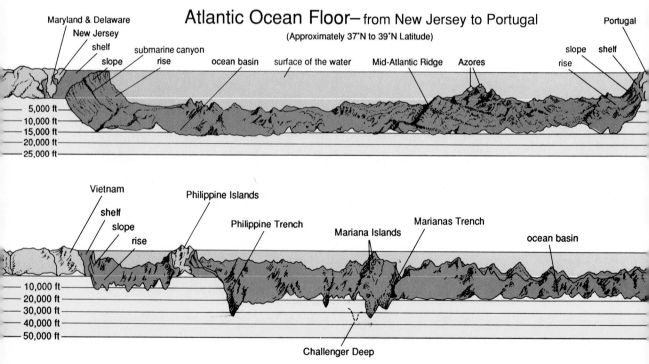

Atlantic Ocean Floor— from New Jersey to Portugal
(Approximately 37°N to 39°N Latitude)

Maryland & Delaware
New Jersey
shelf
submarine canyon
slope   rise   ocean basin   surface of the water   Mid-Atlantic Ridge   Azores
Portugal
slope   shelf
rise

5,000 ft
10,000 ft
15,000 ft
20,000 ft
25,000 ft

Vietnam
shelf
slope
rise
Philippine Islands
Philippine Trench
Mariana Islands
Marianas Trench
ocean basin

10,000 ft
20,000 ft
30,000 ft
40,000 ft
50,000 ft

Challenger Deep

flowed off the continents into the seas. As the slope becomes less steep, you slide along the *continental rise.* At last you come to the deep-sea, to the floor called the *ocean basin.* You stand at the bottom of the sea.

In the Atlantic Ocean you will eventually come to a gigantic range of mountains. Sometimes the mountaintops rise above the surface of the sea as islands, such as the Azores. In the Pacific Ocean the Hawaiian Island Mauna Kea is the top of the highest ocean mountain on the earth. Also in the Pacific you might run into the biggest trench in the world, the Marianas Trench. Mt. Everest would fit into the lowest part–the Challenger Deep–and there would still be a mile and a quarter of ocean over the peak. It is said that if you dropped a steel ball into the Challenger Deep from a ship, the ball would fall through the ocean for sixty-three minutes before it hit bottom.

Also along the bottom you would see long cracks in the seabed and springs bubbling up. Sometimes the springs are like smoky mud gushers called *chimneys,* spewing out rich minerals into the sea. The water coming out of these black stacks can be as hot as 750 degrees Fahrenheit.

Much of what scientists know about the ocean floor comes from *sonar,* a system that measures the time it takes for sound waves to go to the bottom of the ocean and come back. Many sonar readings put together on a graph make a ''picture'' of the lay of the ocean floor.

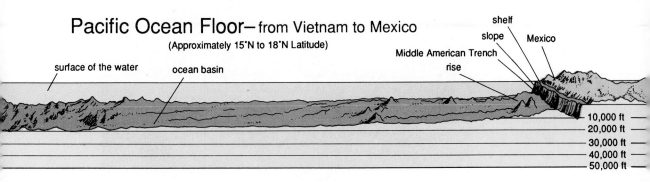

Pacific Ocean Floor–from Vietnam to Mexico
(Approximately 15°N to 18°N Latitude)

surface of the water   ocean basin

shelf
slope   Mexico
Middle American Trench
rise

10,000 ft
20,000 ft
30,000 ft
40,000 ft
50,000 ft

Life in the Sea

In a cup of seawater thrive millions of tiny plants and animals called *plankton*. *Phytoplankton* are microscopic plants. *Zooplankton* are tiny animals. Phytoplankton feed every animal in the sea, directly or indirectly. They drift along the surface, using the energy of the sun to build new plant cells. The zooplankton eat the phytoplankton. Larger animals such as shellfish eat the zooplankton. Still larger animals such as seals eat the shellfish, and seals may become food for killer whales. This food chain all depends on the phytoplankton. Some of the large animals, such as the finback whales, feed directly on plankton.

Phytoplankton are not plants as you probably think of plants. They have no stems, flowers, roots, or seeds. They are bits of living jelly that contain chlorophyll. From a mineral dissolved in seawater, some plankton, the *diatoms,* form a glasslike ''shell.'' Some look like minuscule crystal jewel boxes. Others are like strings of beads, or stars, or propellers. Like all plants, phytoplankton need carbon dioxide, a gas in the air, to grow.

Another phytoplankton sometimes causes a phenomenon called *red tide*. When billions and billions of these tiny red-brown plants roll in together to the

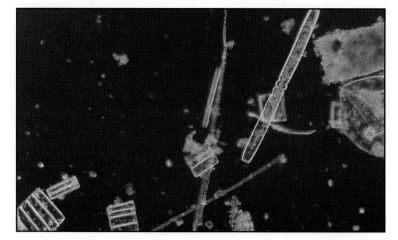

shore, the tide looks red. At night these plankton sparkle, making a beautiful greenish-yellow glow. During a red tide, when they are abundant, they make an intense green shine in the foam of the waves at night.

The largest plant in the ocean is the giant kelp. It can grow one to two feet in a day and can get up to several miles long. Sometimes kelp grow close together in huge beds. Herbivores like snails and sea urchins live among the strands of kelp, sheltered from the sun and supplied with food. Why do you think fishermen know that where there is a kelp bed there will be fish nearby? They know that carnivores will come to the beds to hunt the herbivores. Sea otters, octopuses, and about 200 other kinds of sea creatures frequent the kelp forest.

Do you think you would ever eat seaweed? You probably already have. Kelp, perhaps better known as seaweed, contains the chemical *algin*. At least 300 different manmade products use algin, such as salad dressing, pancake syrup, ice cream, and even chocolate milk. Algin is also used in making things such as toothpaste, car polish, and printer's ink.

If you were in a plane looking down on a giant kelp bed, it would look like a mass of brown weeds floating in the ocean. Under the water, though, the seaweeds seem like a beautiful forest. The canopy is made of fronds, that having grown as tall as they can, now grow sideways under the surface. Sunlight cannot get through the canopy. How then does photosynthesis take place?

Photosynthesis occurs in the tops of the kelp plants. Inside the fronds, microscopic channels transfer the products of photosynthesis to the lower parts of the plant. A kelp plant can live for seven or more years, drawing nutrients from the water and producing its own food through photosynthesis. Some kinds of kelp in the Sargasso Sea, having calm waters and good temperatures, can live for hundreds of years.

For a long time scientists thought that no life existed at the bottom of the seas. Why do you suppose they thought that? With no light and with extreme pressure from miles of water above, the ocean floor would seem to offer little hope for life. Have you ever been under water? How did it feel? And when you got out of the water, did you feel as though you were still moving through water? Imagine the pressure there is ten thousand or thirty thousand feet underwater. What do you think keeps the water from being too cold for life where the sun cannot reach?

In 1960 two men went down into the sea in a *bathyscaphe,* or ''deep boat.'' The *Trieste,* as the bathyscaphe was named, descended into the Marianas Trench 35,800 feet. There in the black depths, lights from the *Trieste* showed something unexpected. The men saw a red shrimp and a foot-long fish that resembles a flounder. They saw life deep under the sea.

INSIDE Information

In 1977, the *Alvin*, another deep-diving craft, went to the deep parts of the Pacific Ocean. And there again, the scientists were astonished to see a variety of life thriving, sealed off from the sun's rays and under tons and tons of water pressure. They saw huge white clams, pink fish, six-foot long red worms, and delicate flowerlike animals called anemones. They saw fish with luminous patches along their sides, pelican eels that can swallow animals three times their size, and angler fish with enormous jaws and ragged, razor-sharp teeth. These animals of the deep have as much pressure inside their bodies as outside, allowing them to live under miles of water. God has carefully designed them to live where they do.

Of all the animals in the sea, the zooplankton are the smallest. Some have skeletons of glassy spikes. Others have soft bodies around chalky skeletons full of little openings like windows. Still others look like microscopic shrimp. What do you think is the largest animal?

The heaviest animal that has ever lived on earth is the great blue whale. It is far bigger than any dinosaur or elephant. It can be one hundred or more feet long and can weigh 150 tons. Only the vast spaces of the sea could hold these creatures. Usually slate blue on top with a white or yellowish underside, the blue whale can blow a spout of water twenty feet high from the blowhole in the top of its head.

INSIDE Information

Whales that live on small sea organisms and have no teeth are *baleen whales. Baleen* are strips of whalebone that hang from the roof of the whale's mouth. These strips strain the plankton and small shrimp and fish from the gallons of seawater the whale takes in. The great blue whale and the humpback whale are two baleen whales. It is remarkable that these giants of the sea live on the smallest plants and animals in the water.

Scientists cannot even guess how many different animals and plants live in the sea. From the dolphins that whistle through the waters to the giant squids over fifty feet long, from the scallop with its hundred bright blue eyes to the flying fish, from the sunfish to the humpback whales singing songs in the deep, the creatures of the seas reveal God's wonderful design in our world.

"They that go down to the sea in ships, that do business in great waters; these see the works of the Lord, and his wonders in the deep." Psalm 107:23-24

Studying the Ocean

Men have always been curious about the seas. They have feared its killer waves, seen the mighty creatures surface from its depths, and watched the surging waters change the shores. Yet *oceanography,* the study of the sea, is a fairly new science.

For the most part, such a study had to wait until appropriate equipment could be made. In the 1600s and 1700s explorers gained new information, attempting to make correct maps of the oceans and shores and to measure currents. But how much do you think men could tell about the ocean by surveying its edges and surface? Scientists also needed to get under the water.

In 1690, a man devised the first workable diving equipment. It was a heavy and clumsy metal bell with an air supply carried in barrels in the top. It allowed men to be underwater for some time, but it could not go very deep. About 150 years later, explorers wore helmeted suits with long pipes that would reach above the surface to allow breathing. One hundred years later still the famous sea explorer Jacques Cousteau introduced the Self-Contained Underwater Breathing Apparatus (scuba). What is the advantage of having tanks of air strapped to a diver's body? The diver can swim about freely, taking his air supply with him.

Today underwater vessels like the *Trieste* and the *Alvin* make the study of the deep much safer and more comfortable than ever before. Some nuclear submarines used in research can travel over 60,000 miles without stopping to refuel. Scientists can get a better view of life in the oceans from deep, lengthy stays than they ever could from the short and far more shallow dives with scuba gear. Can you think of an advantage that scuba divers have over scientists in underwater vessels? Other submarine vessels carry cameras and have mechanical arms that scientists can operate electronically from the surface.

Why do you think men spend so much time and money studying the ocean? Is it just to satisfy a long-lived curiosity? Is it because the seas cover so much of the earth? Both of those reasons have something to do with it. But more importantly, scientists know that the ocean ultimately affects life above its surface. Fishing, weather, shipping, and even whole climates are influenced by the ocean.

By studying the sea, scientists hope to be able to harvest more food, minerals, and perhaps drinkable water from it. At least eighty chemicals and many minerals can be easily taken from seawater now. For example, much of the world's tin is removed from the coastal waters of Thailand and Indonesia. And even more valuable minerals—copper, nickel, gold, and silver—are abundant in oceans. All that is needed is an inexpensive, efficient way to get these treasures.

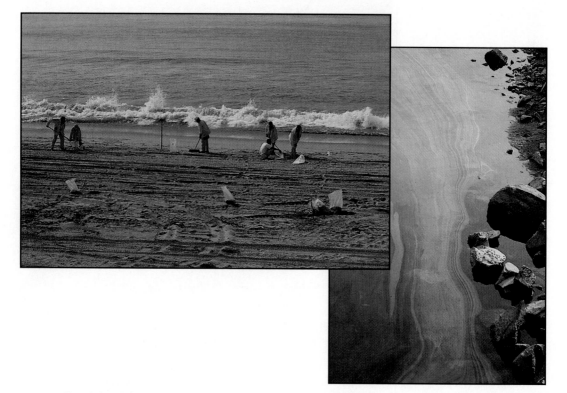

Studying the sea will also help us to use the sea more responsibly. Many continental shelves are rich in oil and gas. Pipelines bring the oil from the offshore rigs to shore. The oil spills you hear about happen when the pipelines break or when tanker ships run into rocks or barriers and tear open. Oceanographers have studied the results such spills have had on animals and plants of ocean and shore. Since natural seepage accounts for most of the oil in the ocean, the studies are not always easy to carry out or interpret properly. No one knows whether much damage occurs over the long term.

Oceanographers have discovered many delicate connections between the ocean currents and animal life. The Peru Current, for example, is usually rich in nutrients. And so it is usually rich in phytoplankton and, thus, in many kinds of fish. But when the springs on the ocean floor that provide the nutrients fail, as they do sometimes, plants and animals die by the millions.

Careful study of such phenomena can teach us much about the connections among all the elements of the sea. And it should also tell us how everything that man does in the sea has far-reaching effects.

Some ocean creatures have been hunted and killed to near-extinction. The narwhal, because its spiraling tusk is a source of ivory, has almost been wiped out. And overfishing in some areas has led to an imbalance in all the populations of fish. Why do you think the loss of one kind of fish causes problems for many other kinds? Oceanography has helped prove to governments around the world that careful use of the oceans and their resources is vital to life on the earth. And it has helped to find some responsible methods of using the sea.

Fish farming is a fairly new idea that is helping balance man's need for food with his responsibility to use the wealth of the sea wisely. Fish farmers grow fish in a protected area without interrupting the cycles of life in the surrounding sea. Fish farming makes it possible to get sea fish to eat without hunting them down in the open sea.

Scientists have found ways to get drinking water from the sea. They use a process called *desalinization,* which means taking the salt out. How are salt and other minerals removed from seawater in nature? Evaporation and condensation can be used in desalinization of plants as well. Seawater is pumped in and boiled or drawn up by the sun. The fresh water is collected and stored. In some plants, seawater is frozen. Ice crystals form from pure water, leaving salt behind.

Oceanographers and other scientists are constantly learning new things about the sea and the life in it. And there is so much left to explore. One deep-sea diver, looking forward to a five-and-a-half mile descent in *Trieste II,* says there is no telling what wonder will be discovered next.

Finding Out . . .

About Desalinization

1. Get some salt water, a beaker, a Bunsen burner, some ice cubes, bent glass tubing, a conical flask with a stopper, and a dishpan.

2. Put the beaker in the dishpan, and put the ice cubes around it. Put the salt water in the flask, put the stopper in the flask, and push one end of the glass tubing into the stopper.

3. As your teacher sets the flask over the Bunsen burner, bring the dishpan closer so that the other end of the glass tubing goes inside the beaker.

4. Watch as your teacher lights the burner under the salt water. What happens as the water gets hot? What do you think will happen to the steam? What happens to the steam? What will happen to the salt? Taste the water in the beaker. Record your observation.

3

Wind

Atmosphere

Almost everyone has asked at some time in his life–"Where does the wind come from?" People used to make up stories to explain the wind. Some stories said that the winds were messengers from the sun. Others said that gentle winds were good spirits and harsh winds were cruel spirits, both always fighting over the earth. We know much more now about wind and how it really comes to be. To understand wind, we must first study air.

Did you know that every day, on every square inch of your body, there are many pounds of air pressing on you? Imagine a one-inch column of air reaching out from your hand to the end of Earth's atmosphere. It weighs about 14.7 pounds. If you have 2,000 square inches of body surface, how much air pressure is pushing on you? 29,400 pounds. What do you think keeps you from being squashed flat under almost fifteen tons of air pressure?

Remember the sea creatures at the very bottom of the oceans? Their inner body pressure matched the pressure of the water against them. We live at the bottom of a "sea of air," and God has designed our bodies so that there is almost as much (or slightly less) pressure pushing out as there is pushing in. The weight of air on the earth is called *atmospheric pressure*. This pressure varies only a little day to day.

Finding Out . . .

About Atmospheric Pressure

1. Get a pint jar, a large balloon, a thick rubber band, a drinking straw, a straight pin, some glue, a toothpick, poster board, a pen, and your notebook.

2. Cut the balloon open and spread it over the mouth of the pint jar. Secure the balloon with the rubber band. Pinch and glue both ends of the straw flat. Glue one end to the middle of the balloon covering. Glue the straight pin to the other end of the straw. Glue the toothpick to the edge of the mouth of the jar so that the straw rests on it.

3. Make a recording card from the poster board, being sure it is taller than the jar. Put the card on a wall out of the sun and where the temperature does not change much.

4. Put the jar where it will not be in the sun. Place the jar so that the pin barely touches the poster board. Mark where the pin points on the card and fill in your notebook page. Check and record the position of the straw for several days. Can you find any patterns between kinds of weather and the atmospheric pressure?

The Troposphere

Like the oceans, air is a great fluid body, with its own currents and streams. The air "ocean" surrounds the earth in layers. We live in the *troposphere,* a layer about seven to nine miles thick. The troposphere is a mixture of gases–mostly oxygen and nitrogen–and microscopic drops of water. Billions and billions of tiny dust particles also drift in the troposphere, kept floating by the slightest movement of air.

Almost all weather happens in the troposphere. For example, the tiny water drops can become clouds and fog. They can also turn into rain and snow, depending on the temperature of the air. Dust helps create red sunsets and sunrises, and certain kinds of dust provide the right conditions for water drops to form clouds. *Tropo* means "to turn" and *sphere* means "circle" or "ball." The troposphere is, you might say, the circle of air that turns with the earth.

The Stratosphere

Above the troposphere, the air is thin and cold. There is little dust and almost no water droplets. This is the *stratosphere,* a layer of air that begins above the troposphere. *Stratosphere* comes from two word parts meaning "covering circle." Within this layer is the *ozone layer,* a band of a special kind of oxygen. The ozone acts like a shield for the earth, keeping out many harmful rays from the sun. Some scientists are worried that pollution that mixes with the ozone will change the oxygen, weakening the protective covering. Other scientists believe that hundreds of electrical storms occurring around the world every day replenish the special oxygen, keeping the shield intact.

What Causes Wind?

Wind is air that is moving across the earth. The great winds that pushed the clipper ships across the oceans and the light breezes that cool you off on the ball field are masses of moving air. But what makes the air move?

The answer involves warm and cold air. The sun heats the earth, keeping our atmosphere suitable for life. The part of the earth facing the sun at any time will be warmer than the part turned away. Thus nights are almost always cooler than days.

The warmer the air, the lower the air pressure, or the less gravity pulls on it. Thus warm air rises. The cooler the air, the greater the air pressure. What do you think happens to air that cools? It sinks. What happens when the earth's surface is warmed by the sun? The air over it warms and rises. What do you think happens to the cooler air in the troposphere? Cooler air moves in to take the place of the rising warm air. This exchange creates a movement in the air, called a wind. Why do you think some winds are more powerful than others?

Part of the reason that not all winds are the same is that the earth heats up more in some places than in others. In fact, that there are winds at all is due to an uneven flow of heat to and from the earth.

You know that the earth is tilted on its axis. That means its axis is not parallel to the sun's axis. The tilt of the earth causes sunlight to hit some places on earth directly and other places at a slant. Where do you think it gets warmer–where sunlight hits directly or at a slant?

More hot air rises from places warmed by direct rays. It rises as far as it can, and then it begins to cool and sink. When the air rises, air that has not been warmed as much rushes under to take its place. You might, then, think of wind as air moving in a circle of hot to cold.

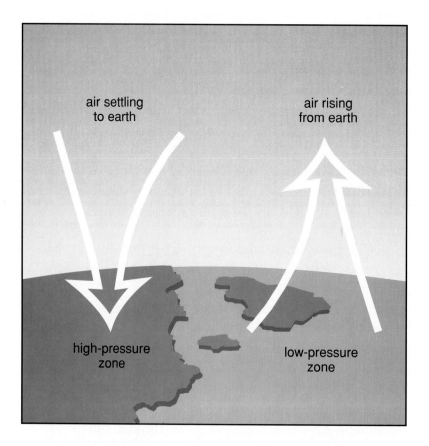

air settling to earth

air rising from earth

high-pressure zone

low-pressure zone

About the Heating of the Earth

1. Get two shoe boxes or baking pans, some soil, two classroom thermometers, a watch, and three bricks or thick books.

2. Fill the pans or boxes with soil to within one inch of the rims. Be sure that they are equally prepared. Measure the temperature of the surface soil in both pans by placing the bulbs of the thermometers in the soils. Record the temperatures. Be sure that the bulbs do not touch the pans.

3. Choose a clear day. Go out at noon and set one box flat on the ground or on the window sill in the direct sunlight. Tilt the other box up on the bricks or books so that the sunlight hits it at an angle. Why should both boxes be in the same area?

4. Leave the boxes in the sunlight for an hour. Record the temperature of the surface soil in each box every fifteen minutes. What can you say about the heating power of direct and slanted sunlight?

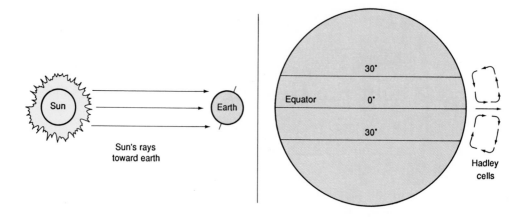

Sun's rays
toward earth

Hadley
cells

Look at the drawing of the earth and sun. Where do you think the most warm air rises from on the earth? Where do you think most of the cool air comes from? Can you guess which way the winds blow over the Atlantic Ocean?

Warm air rises from the equator and then moves out toward the North and South Poles. It cools on the way and sinks and moves back toward the equator. This ongoing process creates a kind of air tunnel around the earth called a *Hadley cell.* There is a Hadley cell on each side of the equator. Do you think these cells move in the same direction or opposite directions?

You have probably heard somewhere that the equator is an imaginary line that divides the Northern and Southern Hemispheres. The line is imaginary in that it is not drawn on our earth. But there is a kind of line– a belt of unmoving air–around the middle of the earth. Why do you think there is little or no wind there? The air at the equator is moving straight up, not across the surface.

"The wind goeth toward the south, and turneth about unto the north; it whirleth about continually, and the wind returneth again according to his circuits."

Ecclesiastes 1:6

If the air on the earth simply rose and fell in big unchanging circles, there would be completely predictable weather everywhere. But as you know, the winds and weather are not on an exact schedule year after year.

If the earth were perfectly smooth and perfectly still, winds might travel in large unwavering circles. But it has mountains and shores and islands, which force the wind to change paths. And the earth rotates. Can you predict what will happen to the arrows representing the Hadley cell when the model earth rotates?

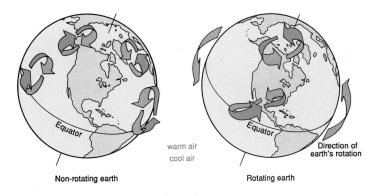

warm air
cool air

Direction of earth's rotation

Non-rotating earth   Rotating earth

The slightly sideways movement of the wind caused by the rotation of the earth is called the *Coriolis effect*. The Coriolis effect explains why winds in the Northern Hemisphere are deflected clockwise. (To think of this movement, pretend you are looking down upon the North Pole.) In the Southern Hemisphere, the winds go counterclockwise. Have you ever noticed that water goes down the drain in a swirl? That swirl shows the Coriolis effect. In the Northern Hemisphere, the water swirls clockwise. What do you think happens in the Southern Hemisphere? What do you think happens at the equator? At the equator, water goes straight down the drain. What does that tell you about the Coriolis effect at the equator?

Finding Out . . .

About the Coriolis Effect

1. Get a vinyl or plastic globe that may be spun on its axis, a medicine dropper, red food coloring, some water, some paper towels, and your notebook.

2. Put some food coloring in a half cup of water. Predict what will happen when you drop some water on the motionless globe. Then squeeze a stream of water from the medicine dropper onto the globe. Record what happens.

3. Then spin the globe. Predict what will happen when you drop water on the spinning globe. Then squeeze some water onto the globe. Record what happens.

4. Compare the pattern of the water drops to air moving. How do you think winds move across the earth? Do you think the rotation of the earth has anything to do with the ocean currents?

Kinds of Winds

The major winds of the earth are called *prevailing winds*. They blow consistently over large areas year after year. Sailors learned about such winds and relied on them. So many merchant or trading ships used the prevailing winds on either side of the equator that these winds became known as the *trade winds*.

The trade winds called *westerlies* blow from the west. In the Northern Hemisphere the paths of the westerlies are broken up by land. In the Southern Hemisphere these winds pass mostly over ocean. Here they blow strong and steady most of the time.

INSIDE Information

Where the two belts of trade winds come together along the equator there are often no trade winds. Can you say why the winds do not blow either east or west there? The air is moving up or down, not across the earth. Sailors soon learned that their sails would droop and their ships would stall in the troughs between the trades. They named these places of bad sailing the *doldrums*. Have you ever heard anyone say he was in the doldrums? What did he mean?

Places of poor sailing also occur on the other side of the trades in the Northern Hemisphere, where the Hadley cell settles out. When the ships got caught in these calms, they were often unable to move for days or even weeks. Sometimes the ships ran out of provisions, and the horses aboard died and had to be thrown into the sea. It seems that so many ships were snared this way that these calms became known as the *horse latitudes*.

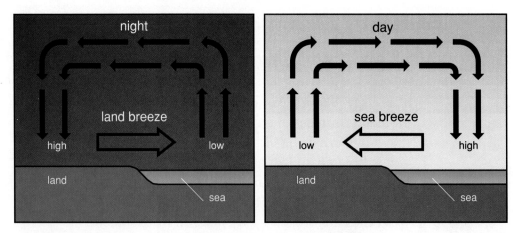

The winds and breezes that you feel as you walk to school or open the windows are produced not by prevailing winds but rather by the local changes in air pressure. *Local winds,* although not as large as or usually as powerful as prevailing winds, are important to living conditions in the immediate vicinity.

Mountain winds and *valley winds* result from a process you already know about. During the day, when air warms up, will it move up the mountain slope or stay in the valley? What will happen when it rises up the mountain? At night what will happen to the air? Where will the cold air go?

Land breezes and *sea breezes* are local winds that occur along coasts and shores. Water absorbs more heat and so does not send as much heat back into the atmosphere as land does. During the day then, where will more air be rising–over land or sea? Over the land. As the air rises, where will cool air come from to take its place? From the sea. Which way will the breeze be blowing during the day? Toward the land.

Water holds heat longer than land. The land quickly sends its heat back into the atmosphere after dark. Where will more warm air be rising then? Over the sea. Where will the cool air come from to replace the rising air? From the land. Which way will the breeze be blowing at night?

Finding Out . . .

About the Heating of Soil and Water

1. Get two pie pans, two thermometers, a graduated cylinder or measuring cup, some water, dry potting soil, and your notebook.

2. Put a measure of soil into one pan but do not fill the pan completely. Put the same amount of water into the other pan. Set both pans in a dark corner of the room until both the soil and water are at the same temperature.

3. Set both pans in full sunlight. Check the temperatures in both pans every twenty minutes. Be sure to measure the temperatures below the soil and water surfaces. Record the time and the temperatures. In an hour, move both pans into the shade. Check and record the temperatures every twenty minutes.

4. What were the differences in temperature between the pans in the checks you made? What do you observe about the rate at which soil and water heat up and cool down?

Describing Wind

Which way is the wind blowing? When scientists answer this question, they name the wind by where it is coming from, not by where it is going. Remember the breezes that occur along shorelines. Is the breeze that comes from the ocean to the land a land or a sea breeze? A sea breeze. How does a land breeze blow?

An easy way to tell which way the winds are blowing is to look at low clouds. They always move with the wind. Another way is to look at a *weather vane*. Perhaps you have seen a weather vane atop a barn or a garage. The arrow points to the direction from which the wind is coming. Why do you think the tail of the arrow must always be bigger than the head?

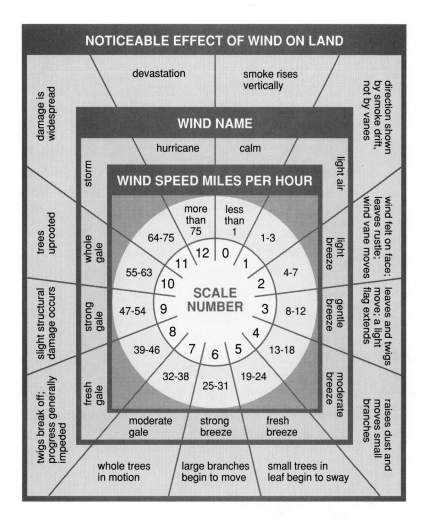

NOTICEABLE EFFECT OF WIND ON LAND

WIND NAME

WIND SPEED MILES PER HOUR

SCALE NUMBER

People also like to know how fast the wind is blowing. You can gauge wind speed in a general way by observing leaves and tree branches and flags. If a flag barely lifts away from the pole, the breeze is light. If whole trees are swaying, a strong wind called a *gale* may be blowing. Scientists measure wind speed with an *anemometer*, an instrument that looks something like a helicopter rotor with cups turned sideways on the blades to catch the wind. A meter attached to the anemometer shows the speed of the wind in miles or kilometers per hour. Look at the chart to compare the wind effects you can see with anemometer readings.

Finding Out . . .

About Wind Direction

1. Get a compass, some poster board, some glue, a glass or wire rod at least three feet long, the cap from a plastic ball-point pen, and your notebook.

2. Cut two arrows from the poster board, using the pattern your teacher gives you. Glue the arrows together, leaving a space unglued as the pattern shows. Slide the opening in the arrow over the pen cap.

3. Go outside. In an open area, push the rod into the ground until it is straight and steady. Put the pen top over the end of the rod. Check to see that the cap can turn easily on the rod. Make sure that the arrow is level. Does the vane show that any wind is blowing? Using the compass, find the direction the wind is blowing. Record your observations.

 # Weather

"Whatsoever the Lord pleased, that did he in heaven, and in earth, in the seas, and all deep places. He causeth the vapours to ascend from the ends of the earth; he maketh lightnings for the rain; he bringeth the wind out of his treasuries."   *Psalm 135:6-7*

When God created the earth, He provided for all the needs of all living things and for all the changes that would come to the world. He planned a world that would continue, orderly and prospering, after a Fall and a Flood. He established the vast cycles of the oceans and the atmosphere; He set in place the seasons; He brought "out of his treasuries" the makings of our weather.

Few things are so universally interesting as the weather. Everyone wants to know—"What will the weather be like?" We want to know how we should dress, when we should plant and harvest crops, where we should travel, if we should carry an umbrella. Weather influences our moods, affects our health, changes our picnic plans, and even sometimes determines where we live. The more you know about weather, the better you can get along in it.

Humidity

You have probably heard someone say, "It's not the heat; it's the humidity." The person was no doubt commenting on the fact that warm, dry air is more comfortable than warm, wet air. Dry air lets perspiration evaporate and cool the body much better than wet, or *humid,* air does.

To describe how "wet" the air is, scientists compare how much water vapor is in the air at a certain temperature with how much water would be in it if it were holding all it could. They call this description *relative humidity.* If air at a certain temperature has half the water vapor in it that it could have, we say that the relative humidity is 50 percent. If the air is holding its limit of water vapor, the relative humidity is 100 percent.

Cool air cannot hold as much water vapor as an equal amount of warm air can. If air is at 100 percent relative humidity, what do you think will happen when the air cools? The air will have more water vapor than it can hold then. You have seen one result many times on a hot summer day. Your glass of iced tea has little drops of water running down its sides. The air around the glass is warm and humid; the air touching the glass has been cooled by the iced tea. The water vapor that cannot be held in the cooler air becomes liquid water on the glass. Bigger demonstrations of air cooling and going past 100 percent relative humidity are dew and– on cold days–frost.

Finding Out . . .

About Humidity

1. Get a wooden tongue depressor, two small dowel pegs, a small wood screw, a felt marker, three long blond human hairs, some glue, a blank 3" × 5" card, a foot-square piece of plywood or fiberboard, and your notebook.

2. Glue one peg about one-half inch in on one end of the tongue depressor. Draw an arrowhead on the other end of the tongue depressor, pointing off the end. Fasten the stick to the square piece of board with the wood screw. Put the screw about two inches down and two inches in from the upper left corner. The arrow on the other end should point right.

3. Glue the other peg ten or twelve inches down the board, making sure it is even with the peg on the tongue depressor. Wrap three long hairs around the peg on the stick and glue them down. Wrap the other end of the hair around the bottom peg, keeping a steady tension in the hair, and glue down.

4. Glue the 3" × 5" card to the board under the pointer so that half the card is above the pointer and half is below it. The pointer should reach just to the middle of the card. Mark where the pointer is pointing and date it.

5. For several days, check and mark the pointer, recording observations in your notebook. What kind of weather makes the pointer go higher? Lower?

Clouds

You learned when you studied winds in the last chapter that warm air rises. You also learned that as air rises, it cools. Now suppose that a bubble of air over a parking lot heats and begins to rise. The rising air is moist. As it rises it begins to cool until it reaches a temperature that cannot hold the amount of water vapor present. What do you think happens?

To find the answer you might go outside and look up at the clouds. Have you ever noticed clouds that look flat on the bottom and fluffy and bright on top? The flat bottom shows the exact place where the water vapor in the rising air started to change into another form of water. We see the liquid (or occasionally frozen water) as a cloud. You can point to the flat bottom of such clouds and say that is just where the temperature in the atmosphere caused the water vapor to change form or to *condense*.

Clouds are masses of water particles floating together in the atmosphere. Dust in the atmosphere is necessary if clouds are to form. The water or ice particles must form around tiny bits of certain kinds of dust. What effect do you think the dirty air over cities has on the number of cloudy days the cities have? Places with dirty air have more cloudy days a year than they did when the air over them was clearer.

Clouds have different shapes, depending on how they are formed. Probably the most well-known cloud is the billowy, puffy, soft-looking *cumulus* cloud. It forms when bubbles of warmed air rise because they are lighter than the air around them. What happens when the warm air cools?

Another kind of cloud forms when great sheets of warm air are pushed up by large masses of cool air. Instead of pockets of air rising to the point where a cloud can form, whole layers of air rise and form a thick cloud layer over much of the sky. These are *stratus* clouds.

Clouds can also be categorized by their height. For example, *cirrus* clouds are very high, 20,000 to 40,000 feet above the earth. They are made of ice crystals and always let light through. These wispy clouds often look like horses' tails or wrinkled strips of gauze. Lower clouds–10,000 to 20,000 feet up–are *alto* clouds.

Finding Out . . .

About Clouds

1. Get a clean peanut butter jar, some very hot water, a tray of ice cubes, a match, a flashlight, and your notebook.

2. Pour about an inch of the hot water into the jar. Strike a match and drop it into the water. Put on the lid. Put the jar in a dark place, such as a closet. Set the tray of ice cubes on top of the jar.

3. Shine the flashlight at the middle of the jar. Record your observations.

Precipitation

When large masses of air suddenly drop in temperature, the water vapor that can no longer be held in the air will condense and may fall as rain, snow, sleet, or hail, all of which scientists call *precipitation.* Not all clouds produce precipitation. For rain or snow to fall, special conditions have to be met.

Air masses have different temperatures and relative humidities. The leading edge of an air mass is called a *front.* The name comes from World War I; it compares moving masses of air to armies at the fronts of battles. When a mass of cold air invades a warm air mass, we talk about a *cold front.* What do you think happens to produce a *warm front?*

Which is heavier–warm air or cold air? Which air mass do you think slides under and pushes the other up when warm and cold fronts meet? The colder air lifts the warm air. Along the slanting line where the fronts meet, warm air rises and cools, forming clouds. When the water drops get too large to stay suspended in the atmosphere, they fall as rain. Sometimes, when the air under the clouds is below freezing, the water drops become solid and fall as sleet.

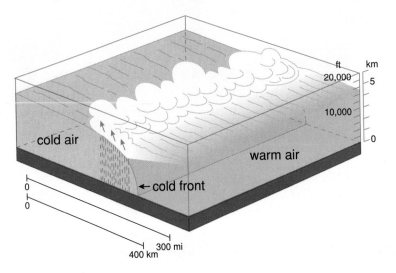

Cold air usually moves along the ground faster than warm air. When both fronts are in an area, the cold air sometimes travels completely under the warm air, lifting the whole warm air mass off the ground. Then a thick layer of stratus clouds forms, which can drop rain over many square miles.

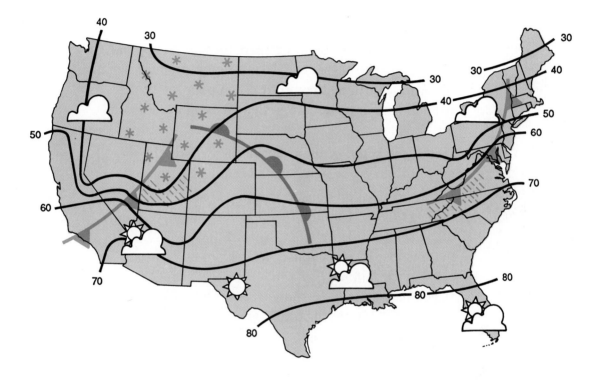

If you look at a weather map on the television or in the newspaper, you can recognize the kind of front in your area by the line used to show it. Cold fronts are represented by lines with triangles along it. Warm fronts are shown by lines with half-circles like little humps along it. Where two fronts meet and neither moves is shown by lines that have both triangles and humps. Which fronts can you find on the map? The symbols always point in the direction that the air mass is moving. Which way is the warm front moving?

Finding Out . . .

About Measuring Rainfall

1. Get a coffee can; a measuring cup; some water; a tall, narrow graduated cylinder; a ruler; and your notebook.

2. Choose an amount of water (perhaps half a cup) and pour it into the coffee can. Measure the depth of the water in the can and record it. Then pour the water from the can into the tall graduated cylinder. Record the depth.

3. Divide the depth of the water in the cylinder by the depth of the water in the can. Record your answer.

4. Put the coffee can outside in an open area. When it rains, bring the can in as soon as the rain stops. Pour the water into the cylinder. Record the depth. Divide that number by the number you recorded in Step 3. How much rain fell?

5. If you happen to have snow, collect the snow in the can. Then let it melt before you measure how much precipitation there was.

Sometimes storms are much more than rain showers that come from clashing cold and warm fronts. When fronts are moving fast as they collide, the collision sometimes sets off a spiraling of air between the fronts. Sometimes the spiral turns into a *tornado,* a whirling windstorm. The speed of the winds can be as high as 250 miles per hour in one of these storms.

Over the oceans in the tropics, another kind of storm brews by gathering warm wet air from the ocean surface. As the warm air rises, towering cumulus clouds–some 10,000 to 20,000 feet tall–form. Heavy rains begin to pour out of the clouds, releasing energy and creating high winds. All these conditions combine into a *hurricane.* To qualify as a hurricane, a storm must have winds over 75 miles per hour. Although a tornado has high winds, it carries no rain.

Before airplanes and weather-tracking computers, hurricanes came smashing across islands and howling into shores without any warning. In 1780, for example, a hurricane swept over Barbados, throwing heavy cannons hundreds of feet, tearing down stone houses, and killing 6,000 people. Today, with modern equipment, weathermen can discover hurricanes forming and can tell people to get ready. In September 1989, weather forecasters warned the people along the southeastern coast of the United States about Hurricane Hugo. People got out of the danger areas, and fewer than fifty died in that major hurricane.

INSIDE Information

The very center of a hurricane, the *eye*, is a vertical tunnel of calm weather. The massive, dark clouds of the storm make a wall around the ten-to-thirty-mile hole in the center of the storm. Hard as it may be to believe, in the middle of whirling, 100-mile-an-hour winds and terrible rains is a place where the sky is clear, the air is warm, and everything is still.

As the eye passes over an area, wrenching winds give way to quiet and calm. Then, twenty or thirty minutes later, the roaring winds and pounding rain strike again. This time, however, the winds and rain are blowing in the opposite direction. Can you think why?

Finding Out . . .

About Storms

1. Get a glass bread pan, some water, red food coloring, and a hot plate. Use only electric heat. Do not do this experiment on your own.

2. Fill the bread pan to within one inch of the top with cool water. Place one end over the burner, turning the burner on low. In the other end, put two or three drops of food coloring.

3. Observe the changes in the water. Record your observations. Compare what happens in the water to what happens in the atmosphere during a storm.

Air Pollution and Weather

In just the last few years, scientists have observed that fish and trees are dying in great numbers in some lakes and forests. No disease or insects seem to be killing them. What then, the scientists want to know, is causing the problem? Some scientists think that part of the problem may be the rain.

Fresh rainwater normally has a slight acid content. When the rain falls it mixes with the carbon dioxide in the air and forms a mild acid called *carbonic acid*. The rain then is only a little more acidic than the milk you drink. On a special scale for measuring acid strength it measures between 5 and 6, which is almost neutral. The lower the number on this scale, the stronger the acid. Carbonic acid is useful because it helps weather rocks into soil.

Rain that falls through polluted air, however, mixes with and washes out many substances that become poisonous when combined with water. What scientists call *acid rain* results. Some such rainwater has an acid content almost like dill pickle juice. On the scale it can measure between 3 and 5. What effect do you think such rain has on plants and fish?

Many scientists believe there is not enough information to draw conclusions from. The records on the lakes in question, for example, go back only about sixty years. How can we know whether the acidic levels are not just part of a much larger cycle of change in the lakes? And not everyone agrees about where the pollution comes from or what is the best way to clean the air. Some of the solutions tried earlier–such as higher smokestacks and filters–only made the problem worse. Some filters held out harmless ash and allowed more deadly acids through. The taller stacks put pollution into higher, thinner air where it spread more quickly over more land.

Perhaps careful study can help cities avoid making such mistakes again. Because God gave us the stewardship of this earth, we must learn all we can about the cycles and processes He established in it. We are responsible to use the treasures of the earth wisely, to work within the limits God has set and not against them. All things are not ours, but God's. We must try, then, to be good caretakers until our Lord returns.

Finding Out . . .

About Air Pollution

1. Get three plain shallow dishes or plates, some clear gelatin powder, some water, some litmus paper, a coffee can or large glass beaker, and your notebook.

2. When your area has a clear forecast for two or three days, mix the clear gelatin as directed on the box. Spread a thin layer on each dish or plate. Set the plates in different places outside. Check on them in two or three days. Be sure to mark each dish before you take it back inside so that you know where it came from. What places seem to be dirtier than others? Can you say why there are differences?

3. On a rainy day, collect rainwater in a coffee can or beaker. Bring the rainwater inside and test it with litmus paper. How much acid is in the water? Record all your observations.

 # Flight

"If I take the wings of the morning, and dwell in the uttermost parts of the sea; Even there shall thy hand lead me, and thy right hand shall hold me."

Psalm 139:9-10

Through the ages, men have always wanted to fly. They devised myths about men who tried to fly, such as Icarus who covered himself with wax and feathers. He flew so close to the sun that the wax melted, his feathers dropped off, and he fell to the earth. They dreamed of taking fantastic voyages around the world and even to the moon. But these flights remained only dreams, and it seemed they would always be dreams. Men could not get off the ground because they did not understand the physical forces affecting flight.

Lift and Weight

Four primary forces affect flight. They are divided into pairs, but the two forces in each pair are opposite to each other. The forces that men had to learn about first were gravity and *lift*. You probably know about gravity. It is the force that keeps everything on the ground. If man wants to fly, he must conquer this force with lift. How would you try to create lift?

Men first tried to produce lift by copying the way birds fly. But these experiments taught them a lot more about gravity and its results than about lift. Many people put feathers on their bodies and jumped from towers, castles, and anything else that was high enough. One man named ibn-Firnas jumped from a building, wearing feathers and wings. He fell quickly to the ground. The person who wrote about this fall said that ibn-Firnas fell because he had no tail. Although many others tried to fly this way, none succeeded, and many were injured.

Others built machines that had birdlike wings. The pilot would either flap the wings himself or use an engine to flap them when he wanted to fly. But these contraptions never got off the ground. About all they ever did was hop around and stir up a lot of air.

By trying to copy birds, men actually took longer to build something that could fly. Why would it take longer to find a way to fly if men tried to copy the way birds fly? Men could only copy how wings look, but not how they worked because they did not understand how complicated birds' wings are. A bird gets most of its lift from the way its feathers work in the air. Each feather has a separate muscle and a special shape. Scientists know much more about bird flight today, but they still do not understand exactly how feathers work. After trying for hundreds of years to fly like birds, men finally gave up. Man might be able to fly, they reasoned, but not like birds.

For a long time men thought of the atmosphere as just empty space; therefore, they had problems thinking of other ways to produce lift. In 1643 a man named Torricelli invented the barometer. This invention proved that air has weight and that it is a substance. After this discovery about air, men began to think more about new ways they could fly. The Montgolfiers, two French brothers, noticed how smoke rose from a fire. Although they did not understand why it rose, they wondered if they could use smoke to create enough lift to fly.

In the summer of 1783 the Montgolfier brothers made the first hot-air balloon. At first they let it fly by itself. Then they put some animals in it. The animals survived. So on November 21, 1783, two men rode in a Montgolfier balloon and became the first to fly. Man had finally conquered gravity. But he still wanted to go wherever he wished and not just where the wind blew him. To be able to do this, he needed to fly in something that was heavier than air.

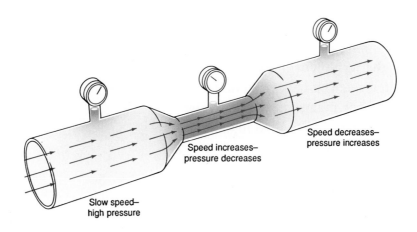

Speed decreases–
pressure increases

Speed increases–
pressure decreases

Slow speed–
high pressure

Problems arose with every experiment. A balloon filled with hot air was lighter than the air around it, and it rose easily. However, it was much more difficult to create lift for something that was heavier than air. At times the problems seemed impossible to overcome. People even began to say that man could never fly in a heavier-than-air craft.

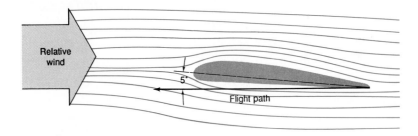

Relative wind

5°

Flight path

A heavier-than-air craft must produce lift with its *airfoils*. The most important airfoil that an aircraft uses to make lift is the wing. Most people thought that the wing produced all its lift by its *angle of attack*. The angle of attack is the angle that the wing has to the wind blowing against the plane as it moves forward. Wind that blows opposite to the direction the plane is flying is called *relative wind*.

If you have ever put your hand outside the window while you were riding in a car, you have seen how angle of attack creates lift. When you turn your hand up, the wind hits the bottom of your hand and forces it up. When you turn your hand down, the wind hits the top of your hand and forces it down.

Have you ever flown a kite? Kites get their lift from the same force that makes your hand go up and down. As you hold the string, the wind blows against the kite and holds it up. Kites were invented by the Chinese long ago and used for many purposes. But few people ever thought that kites might hold some secrets about man's flight.

Then some inventors started making gliders that were like kites. They worked better than the wing-flapping machines of the past. But scientists soon found that an airfoil could get much more lift if they used Bernoulli's principle.

Back in 1738, a Swiss scientist named Daniel Bernoulli had discovered that when a liquid flows faster across a surface, the liquid puts less pressure on that surface. This idea is called *Bernoulli's principle*. It took men several years to discover that air acted a lot like water. When they did, they could start thinking differently about how a wing could create lift.

Finding Out . . .

About Bernoulli's Principle

1. Get a piece of notebook paper, books, a drinking straw, a staight pin, an empty spool, and some stiff paper.

2. Place the edge of a piece of notebook paper inside the cover of a book, letting the rest of the paper hang down over the top of the book. Hold the bottom of the book on your chin close to your mouth. Blow across the top of the book. What happens to the paper?

3. Place two one-inch-thick books at least five inches apart on the edge of a table. Place a sheet of notebook paper on top of both books, letting it sag a little. Use a straw to blow underneath the paper. What happens to the paper?

4. Cut some stiff paper to be 5 cm square. Put a straight pin through the middle of the paper. Put the spool over the pin and hold the paper close to the spool. Blow for a few seconds through the hole in the spool. After you begin blowing, let go of the paper. Why does the paper behave the way it does?

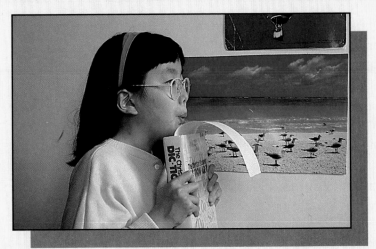

How does an airfoil on an airplane use the Bernoulli principle? The top of the wing is curved more than the bottom, and the air passing over the wing has a greater distance to travel than the air traveling under it. Experiments show that the air going on the top and on the bottom of a wing reaches the back of the wing at the same time. Does the air flow faster over the airfoil or under it?

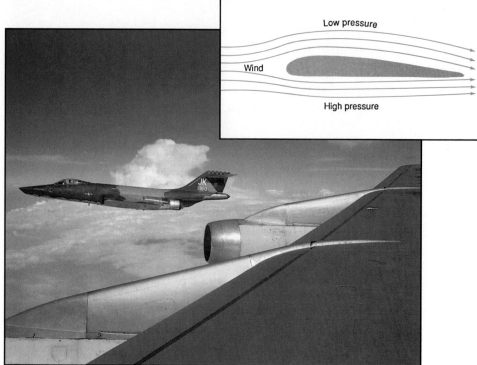

If Bernoulli's principle is correct, the air will flow faster over the top of the wing. Will the air on top of the wing have a high or low pressure? Why does the airfoil rise? It rises because there is more pressure now underneath than there is above.

Many inventors experimented with the shape of airfoils. Soon, people were gliding long distances from hills. They experimented with ways to make gliders easier to control in flight. But one problem remained. People still could not fly wherever they wanted.

Reaction

Action

Thrust and Drag

Men still needed to find a way to create *thrust*.
Gliders flew only short distances, and balloons were too
slow. The gliders needed to have thrust, the force of
flight that makes a plane go forward. *Newton's third
law of motion* describes how airplane engines can
produce thrust. This law says that for every action there
is an equal and opposite reaction. When propellers or jet
engines push air backwards, the plane goes forward.
Have you ever seen a water sprinkler that whirls
around? How does that demonstrate Newton's third law
of motion? The water spurting out one way pushes the
sprinkler head the other way.

Finding Out . . .

About Newton's Third Law

1. Get a balloon and a large ball.
2. Sit in a swing that is not moving. Throw a ball away from you. What happens?
3. Blow up a balloon and hold it tight with one hand. Let the balloon go. Why does the balloon fly away?
4. Blow up the balloon again and ask a friend to hold it tight. Hold one hand above it and your other hand below it. Have your friend let the air out of the balloon. Which way is the action? Which way is the reaction?

The force opposite to thrust is called *drag*. Thrust is the force that makes the plane go forward. Drag is the force that holds the plane back. Drag is mainly by the shape of the airplane and by lift. For the plane to go forward, thrust must exceed, or be greater than, drag.

It was difficult to build an engine that could produce enough thrust without being very heavy. Why do you think this would cause a problem? If any of the four forces change when an airplane is flying, the other forces will also change. Engines add much weight to the airplane. What force would have to be increased to make up for the increased weight? Lift would have to be increased.

But increasing lift makes more drag. What force has to be increased to make up for the increased drag? Increasing that force, however, would put the inventors right back where they started: they needed a more powerful engine, which meant a heavier engine, to make up for the added weight. It seemed that the problem with engines would never be solved.

Success at Last

In 1902 two inventors, Wilbur and Orville Wright, perfected their glider. In just a few short years, they had become famous for their knowledge of flight. They had experimented with their gliders for three years, and in 1903 they decided to add an engine.

They looked many places for an engine, but nobody could make one that was light enough and strong enough. They finally decided that they would make their own engine. With the help of their assistant, they made an engine in six weeks that was better than what they had wanted.

In December of 1903, the Wright brothers made the first powered airplane flight. That first flight went only 120 feet and lasted only 12 seconds, but they kept experimenting. The flights grew longer in time and distance. They had succeeded in their struggle to fly.

Putting It All Together

Although the Wright brothers had succeeded, flying was still risky because the planes were light and difficult to guide. Pilots today have much more control over what their airplanes do. The forces affecting flight are the same as they were then, but the designs of today's airplanes are not.

Pilots can change the amount of lift their wings produce in three ways. They can change the wings' angle of attack; they can change the amount of air that passes over the wings; and they can change the shape of the wing. You have already seen what happens when an object's angle of attack is changed. Pilots can change the angle of attack by pointing the nose of the airplane up or down. If the pilot keeps increasing the angle of attack, will the plane continue to climb?

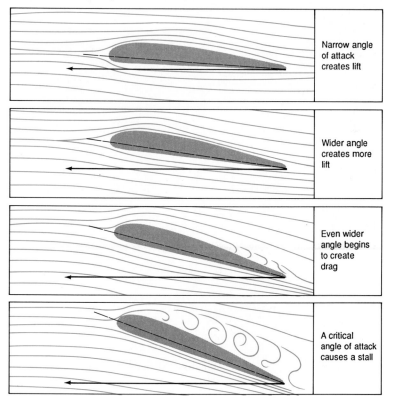

Narrow angle of attack creates lift

Wider angle creates more lift

Even wider angle begins to create drag

A critical angle of attack causes a stall

The wing will create more lift until it reaches the *critical angle of attack,* a point where the air no longer flows smoothly over the top of the wing. As the air tries to follow the top of the wing, it begins to swirl around. This makes a high pressure area on the top of the wing. The wing stalls, or stops producing lift. Then the airplane falls. What should the pilot do to recover from a stall?

However, you may have seen some planes flying straight up. How can they do that without stalling? Planes that can fly straight up are usually very fast. If a plane is fast enough, the relative wind will be flowing over the wing in whatever direction the plane is flying. The wind you would feel if you were standing still does not always blow in the same direction as the relative wind does.

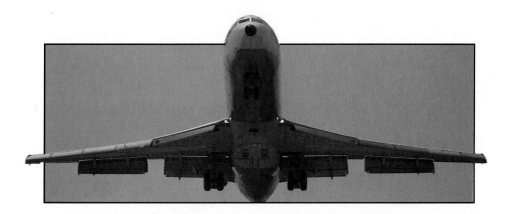

The pilot can also change the amount of air that travels over the wing in order to change the amount of lift. When a plane takes off, how does the pilot cause more air to flow over the wing?

Finally, the pilot can change the shape of the wing. If lift is created because the top of the wing is longer than the bottom, what can the pilot do to the wing to make even more lift? Airplane designers put *flaps* and *ailerons* on the back of the wing so that the pilot can change its shape. Putting the flaps down makes the top of the wing longer and creates more lift. Can you think of a time that an airplane would need the extra lift that flaps can give?

Remember that increasing a plane's air speed or its wings' angle of attack gives it more lift. So most of the time the plane would not need the flaps when it takes off. But when a plane lands, it needs to go slowly, and it needs to point its nose down. Therefore, the flaps are helpful here because they give extra lift when the plane needs to travel at slow speeds.

The pilot uses the ailerons for turning the airplane. The ailerons are connected so that when one goes up, the other goes down. Would the lift be increased or decreased on a wing if the aileron went up? What about if it went down? How would the ailerons make the plane turn left?

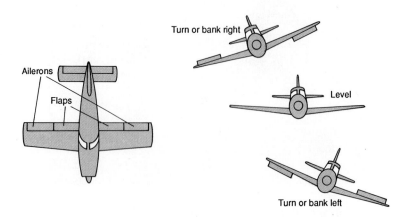

Turn or bank right

Ailerons

Flaps

Level

Turn or bank left

Most planes have two airfoils on the tail. One is called the *vertical stabilizer*. The vertical stabilizer helps to keep the plane's nose from pointing left or right when the pilot wants to fly straight. The pilot uses the *rudder* on the vertical stabilizer to make the plane turn more smoothly. He controls the rudder with his feet and pushes it in the same direction he is turning. The rudder makes the tail follow the turn easily. How does it make the nose point in a different direction?

The *horizontal stabilizer* is the other airfoil on the tail of the plane. This airfoil keeps the nose of the plane from pointing up or down when the pilot wants to fly level. *Elevators* on the back of the horizontal stabilizer allow the pilot to point the nose up or down. How do the elevators at the back of the plane allow the pilot to control the direction that the nose points?

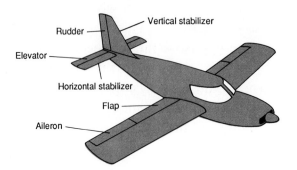

Vertical stabilizer

Rudder

Elevator

Horizontal stabilizer

Flap

Aileron

Once the Wright brothers solved the problem of powered flight, engines became more powerful and complex, and planes traveled faster. Today, some jet-powered planes can reach speeds up to three times the speed of sound–almost 2,000 miles per hour. Why are jet engines so much more powerful than propeller engines?

More powerful engines alone would not help the plane go very much faster. Drag makes it more difficult for the plane to go fast. If the drag can be decreased, the plane will be able to fly faster. How can drag be decreased if most of it is caused by the airplane moving through the air? Engineers decrease drag by *streamlining* the plane. How would you make a plane more streamlined?

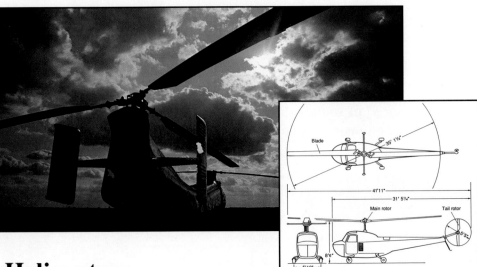

Helicopters

While many men were trying to perfect airplane flight, some were saying that the best way to fly would be straight up. In 1941, Igor Sikorsky finally perfected a machine that could fly not only straight up but also straight down. It could also hover in one place and fly backward and forward and sideways.

A helicopter has two airfoils called *rotors*. Each rotor has several blades that are shaped like long, skinny wings. The rotor must provide both the lift and the thrust for the helicopter.

With only two rotors, how can helicopters fly the way they do? The small rotor on the tail only keeps the helicopter from spinning. How does the tail rotor keep the helicopter from spinning? The pilot can also make the helicopter rotate either left or right if he makes the tail rotor spin different speeds.

How can the large rotor create both lift and thrust? As it spins, it creates lift the same way airplane wings do. As the blades spin, air passes over them and lift is created. What can the pilot do to change the amount of lift the rotor creates so that the helicopter can go up or down? The rotor blades can change their angle of attack (usually called *pitch*) to change the lift. Or the blades

can spin faster so that more air will pass over them. Usually the pilot changes both the pitch and the speed of the rotor blades at the same time.

How do you think the large rotor produces thrust when the pilot wants to fly in a certain direction? If the pilot wants to go forward, he must make the large rotor provide the thrust. To do this, he uses a control stick that makes the whole rotor tilt forward a little bit. When the rotor is tilted forward, it can pull the helicopter both up and forward.

Would it be dangerous for the engine to stop in a helicopter? Many people think that if the rotors stop, a helicopter will fall straight to the ground. However, helicopters can use *autorotation* to fall more slowly. *Auto* means "self"; what do you think *autorotation* means? When the rotor turns with the engine stopped, people say it autorotates. As the engine stops, the helicopter begins to fall. The rotor begins to turn by itself because of the unequal pressures on the blades caused by the wind blowing around them. As the blades spin, what force do they create? How does autorotation slow the fall of a helicopter?

ACTION   Aerospace Engineering

Anyone who helps design, build, test, or operate any machine that travels in space or in the atmosphere is called an aerospace engineer. And every aerospace engineer needs to know many sciences.

Designers and builders especially need to understand the properties of matter. They not only need to be able to choose the right material for construction but also to understand how those materials will act under different conditions. A metal that works well on the ground may not respond correctly in the colder temperatures of high altitudes.

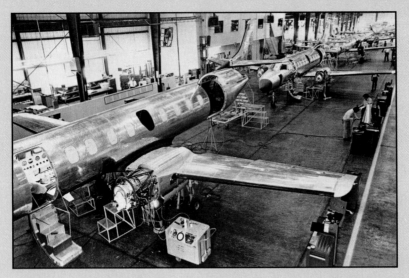

Aerospace engineers also must study energy, including electricity and heat. They must understand weather and the human mind and body. Pilots also need to know astronomy, navigation, mathematics, as well as geography. Why do you think a pilot needs to know all these sciences?

From what you know about the properties of air and water, can you say why underwater travel is included in aerospace engineering?

Finding Out . . .

About Autorotation

1. Get your notebook and a pair of scissors. Cut the pattern out and fold it, following the directions.
2. Drop the helicopter from various heights. Determine from what height the helicopter flies best.
3. Change the shape of the rotors by folding or cutting them. Change the weight by adding paper clips to the bottom part of the helicopter.
4. What causes the helicopter to fall slowly? How does changing the shape of the rotors or adding weight affect the way the helicopter falls? Record your observations.

Flying Today

Flying has changed greatly since the time of Orville and Wilbur Wright. In 1903, the first airplane flew 120 feet before it came back to earth. In 1927, Charles Lindbergh flew *The Spirit of St. Louis* from New York City to Paris without stopping. He was the first ever to make that trip, and it took him over thirty-three hours to fly it. Now people can fly that distance in less than seven hours. In 1986, an airplane named *Voyager* flew around the world without stopping.

Because of these improvements, flying is much more complicated today than it was then. Fifty years ago, airports were often nothing more than a grass landing strip and a hangar, the special building used for storing airplanes. Today large airports are like small cities with everything from fire stations to restaurants and gift shops.

Besides more advanced planes, probably the biggest change in flying is the increased government control. As more people and planes began to fly, the possibility of accidents increased, and some control was needed. The *Federal Aviation Administration* (FAA) was created to make the rules for flying in the United States.

The FAA has designed a very complex system of controlling air traffic. It has established a nationwide network of special radios that helps the pilot know where he is. It has divided the air into special areas with different rules for flying in each area. Without these controls, the sky would be a dangerous place to travel. But today, traveling by air is one of the safest forms of transportation.

Molecules and Atoms

What do a watermelon, a horse, a cherry soda, an emerald, and a bubble have in common? They are all *matter;* that is, they all take up space and have weight. Some of the things take up more space and weigh more than others, but they are all matter.

How is a cherry soda different from a horse? Are they the same color? Do they smell the same? How is a watermelon different from an emerald? Do they taste the same? Which one is harder? Which one do you think would float?

When you describe something, you usually talk about its *properties.* One property of matter is color; another is smell; another is buoyancy, or how well it floats. Other properties are hardness, taste, and weight.

Atomic Theory of Matter

There are several ideas about how matter is made up. Some scientists are investigating the notion that matter is another kind of energy. Other scientists think that matter is made of small particles that are constantly moving. They think of these small particles as resembling incredibly little solar systems, with specks of matter ''orbiting'' a center. These invisible systems are called *atoms,* and the idea that all matter is made of them is the *atomic theory of matter.*

Scientists who accept the atomic theory of matter say that all matter is made of combinations of atoms, called *molecules.* If you could grind one grain of sugar, for example, into a thousand tiny molecules, each tiny piece would still taste like sugar and dissolve like sugar–because those pieces would *be* sugar molecules.

The combinations of atoms give matter its properties. A molecule of sugar is made of carbon, oxygen, and hydrogen atoms. If they are separated, the sugar molecule will no longer exist. A molecule of water is one atom of oxygen and two atoms of hydrogen. If the atoms in a molecule of water are separated, they will no longer have the properties of water.

When matter is made of only one kind of atom, that matter is called an *element*. Oxygen and hydrogen are two elements. God fashioned many elements, tiny building blocks that form all the materials on earth.

Atoms are made of even smaller particles: *protons, neutrons,* and *electrons.* These tiny parts form all the elements. No one has ever really seen inside atoms, however. The parts are so small no magnification we have can make them visible. If an atom could be magnified to the size of a football field, the electron would be the size of a football. That would require a magnification of one hundred trillion (one hundred million million). So any ideas we have about atoms are theories, not true science. And any models that artists draw of the atom are only guesses about how an atom might look.

Every atom except hydrogen seems to have a *nucleus* that contains neutrons and protons. A lithium atom, for example, has three protons and four neutrons in its nucleus. Also, every atom has electrons traveling around the nucleus. The number of electrons is the same as the number of protons. How many electrons does a lithium atom have?

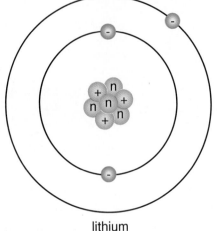

lithium

Atoms also seem to have other pieces or *particles* in their make-up, perhaps as many as a hundred different ones. The atom is far more complex than any model can show or any scientist can fully understand. Even the tiny atom shows God's marvelous power of creation and His infinite wisdom.

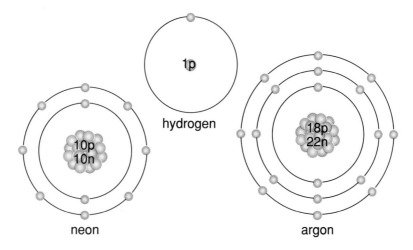

hydrogen

neon

argon

The protons in an atom have an electrical charge called *positive*. Electrons have an electrical charge called *negative*. Neutrons have no charge. If an atom gains electrons, it is negatively charged. What can you say about an atom that is positively charged? But if an atom has the same number of electrons and protons, the atom is not charged, because the negative and positive charges are balanced.

All protons are exactly alike; all neutrons are exactly alike; all electrons are exactly alike. Atoms are different from each other only because they are different combinations of protons, electrons, and neutrons. An atom with one proton and one electron will always be a hydrogen atom. It will act like hydrogen. And it will never be confused with atoms that have more protons and electrons.

Each kind of atom has a symbol that chemists use instead of the whole name. Sometimes the first letter of the name is the symbol. The letter is always a capital. *H* is the symbol for hydrogen, and *O* is the symbol for oxygen. Sometimes two letters from the name make the symbol, as in *He* for helium. Other elements use letters from the Latin names. Iron is called *ferrum* in Latin; so its symbol is *Fe*. When there are two letters, the first is a capital, and the second is lower case.

Finding Out . . .

About Atoms

1. Get three colors of paper, a hole punch, a black pen, and your notebook.

2. Punch at least a dozen holes from each color of paper. Choose one color to be the electrons and label those circles with a minus sign front and back. Choose a color to be the protons and label each of those pieces with a plus sign front and back. Leave the third color, the neutrons, unmarked.

3. Following your teacher's instructions, form models of different atoms. Then form models of atoms on your own, and ask a classmate to identify them.

4. Can you think of a way to make a three-dimensional model of an atom?

How Atoms Behave

Atoms cannot be seen, even with the most powerful microscopes. There are more than 200 trillion in the period at the end of this sentence. One drop of water has billions of water molecules in it. In fact, if a drop of water were magnified until it were the size of the earth, every molecule in it would be the size of an orange. How many oranges do you think it would take to fill up the earth? Just imagine then how many oxygen and hydrogen *atoms* are in that drop of water and how hard they would be to study. But we can understand certain things about atoms by studying molecules.

Molecules are always moving. Sometimes they move differently than at other times. Suppose you had two dozen marbles on a table. If the marbles were rolling around, they would bump into one another. How would putting them in a bowl change their movement? If they could still roll around, they would bump into one another more often than they did on the table.

Molecules tend to move from a place that is crowded to a place that is less crowded. As they do, they "bump" into one another. The molecules keep bumping into one another and moving until they are evenly spaced in the less crowded area. The bigger the area the more the molecules are able to space themselves. Steam, for example, is water; the difference is that the water molecules in steam have spread out through the air instead of sticking more closely together as they do in liquid water. What do you think makes the molecules in steam spread apart?

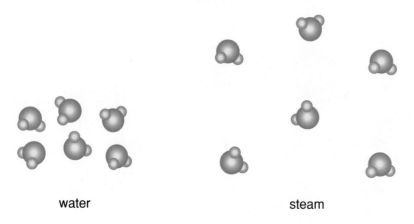

water   steam

Heat and cold can change the way molecules move. Do you think heat slows down or speeds up the movement of molecules? Why do you think so? What do you think makes steam? What do you think cold does to the movement of most molecules? How do you think the molecules in steam compare to the molecules in ice?

Matter can be a *solid,* a *liquid,* or a *gas.* Matter is usually in one of these *states.* If you make water molecules very cold, the matter–water–changes from a liquid to a solid–ice. Changing the space that molecules move in also changes the state of the matter that the molecules form. What happens if you give the water molecules a larger place to escape to and heat them at the same time?

About Molecules

1. Get a small funnel, a wide-mouthed jar, a balloon, and a bottle of cologne.

2. Using the funnel, put a few drops of cologne into the balloon. Blow up the balloon and knot it tightly. Smell inside the jar. What does it smell like? Work the balloon snugly into the mouth of the jar. Leave it for twenty minutes.

3. Remove the balloon. Predict what has changed. Smell inside the jar. Record your observations. What can you infer from your observations? How did the scent of the perfume get from inside the balloon into the jar? What property of perfume do the molecules most obviously carry?

Finding Out . . .

About How Molecules Move

1. Get two beakers, some ink or food coloring, an eye dropper, some hot water, and some cold water.

2. Pour the hot water into one beaker and the cold water into the other. Fill each beaker about three-quarters full. Add one drop of ink or food coloring to each beaker.

3. Predict where the color will spread most quickly. Observe the beakers. How long does it take for the color to spread evenly in each beaker? How could you make the dye in each beaker spread at the same rate?

How Warm Matter Takes Up More Space

1. Get an empty soft drink bottle, a quarter, and some water. You will also need to use a refrigerator freezer.

2. Uncap the bottle and put it in the freezer for ten minutes. When you are nearly ready to take the bottle out, put a drop of water on the quarter and spread it over the surface. Then remove the bottle from the freezer and lightly run a wet finger around the bottle rim.

3. Put the quarter on top of the bottle, wet side down. (The water helps to make a seal.) Observe the quarter for several minutes.

4. Record what happens. Why do you think that the quarter moved? What do you think would happen if the bottle were warmed up faster? What would happen if the coin were smaller?

How Atoms Combine

Everything in the universe is either an element or a combination of two or more of the elements that God created. Scientists can cause a few nonnatural elements to form in laboratories. They can force particles from one atom's nucleus into another atom, forming an atom that does not exist in nature. But the atoms formed this way would never last long under normal conditions.

In nature, some atoms can combine to form molecules. Some molecules can join to form material different from either of the separate molecules. Water molecules form when an oxygen atom joins two hydrogen atoms.

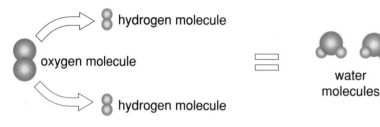

In an atom, the electrons seem to travel around the nucleus in different "orbits." The first orbit can hold only two electrons. So if the atom has three electrons, one electron must go into the next orbit, which holds up to eight electrons. How many "empty slots" would that leave on the second orbit? It would leave seven in this case. Or you can think of it as having one electron to share. The third orbit can hold as many as eighteen electrons. The "slots" on the outside orbit that are not filled make an atom able to join other atoms.

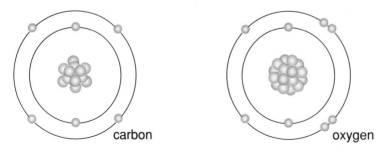

You know that hydrogen has one electron and that oxygen has eight. Can you figure out why a water molecule has two hydrogen atoms and one oxygen atom? How many "empty slots" does an oxygen atom have in its second orbit? It has two. How many hydrogen atoms would have to share electrons with an oxygen atom to fill the second orbit of the oxygen?

INSIDE Information

Atoms with many electrons have a special order for filling the third orbit and all orbits after that. When an atom has filled the first and second orbits, it can gain up to eight electrons in the third orbit. Then the next two electrons must go into the fourth orbit before the third orbit can be completed. The next electrons gained then go into the third orbit. How many more electrons can go into the third orbit? Ten more can go into that orbit because it holds eighteen. Then the fourth orbit can take six more–until it has eight. Where do the next two electrons go?

How Molecules Combine

1. Get half a pint of whipping cream, a beaker, and a jar with a tight lid. You will also need a means of keeping the cream cold until you use it.

2. Pour the cream into the clean jar and close the lid securely. Describe the cream.

3. Shake the jar vigorously for ten minutes. You may want to take turns with a partner. Shake the jar until a solid has formed. Then shake the jar some more.

4. Open the jar and pour the liquid into the beaker. Observe the solid in the jar and the liquid in the beaker. Compare each to the description you made of the cream earlier. What molecules have formed a solid? What molecules have been separated from the cream? Do you think that all the water molecules have been separated from the butterfat molecules? Taste the solid. If you keep it cool, you can use the cream at dinner.

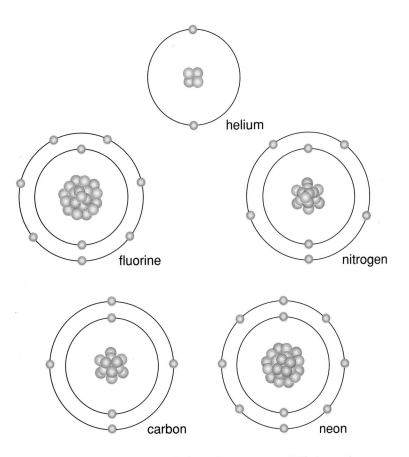

helium

fluorine

nitrogen

carbon

neon

Some atoms do not join other atoms. Look at the models of the helium and the neon atoms. Can you discover a reason that helium and neon do not combine with any other atoms in any way under natural conditions?

How many electrons does helium have? And how many electrons does it take to fill the first orbit? Because helium has just enough electrons to fill an orbit completely, we say that the orbit is *closed*. That is, the atom does not have electrons to share or spaces for other atoms' electrons to fill.

What can you say about the neon atom? Is the second orbit closed? How do you know? Look at the other models of atoms on this page. Would any of them act like the helium and neon atoms?

Representing Atoms in Formulas

When scientists write about combinations that atoms make, they use the atomic symbols and numbers to make *formulas*. The formula for water is H_2O and the formula for salt is NaCl. Since you know what atoms make up both of these molecules, see whether you can discover what the formulas tell about the molecules.

The symbols tell you what atoms are in the molecule. What atoms are in water? What atoms are in

Atoms in a Periodic Table

(the first eighteen elements in the periodic table)

1 **H** hydrogen ← number of electrons ← symbol ← name				
3 **Li** lithium	**4** **Be** beryllium	**5** **B** boron	**6** **C** carbon	**7** **N** nitrogen
11 **Na** sodium	**12** **Mg** magnesium	**13** **Al** aluminum	**14** **Si** silicon	**15** **P** phosphorus

salt? The numbers tell you how many of each atom are in the molecule. Water, for example, has two hydrogen atoms (H_2) and one oxygen atom. What can you say about the formula for salt?

Look at these formulas. Using the chart of elements, tell what you know about the molecules represented.

- $C_{12}H_{22}O_{11}$ Cane sugar
- CO_2 Carbon dioxide
- $NaHCO_3$ Baking soda

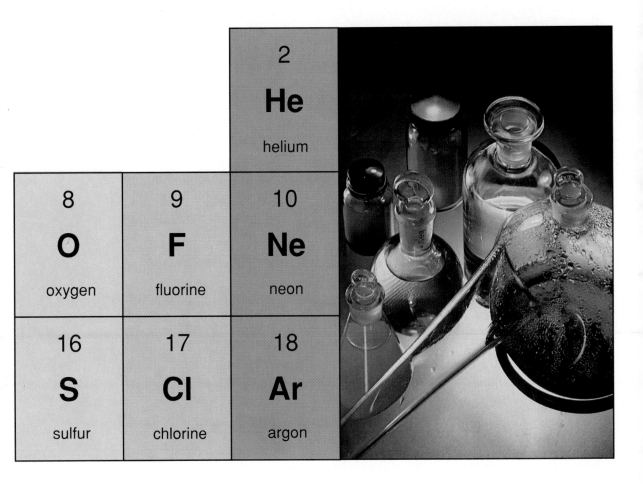

How Much Matter in an Atom?

Although an atom has a nucleus of protons and neutrons surrounded by electrons, most of the atom is empty space. Imagine that the nucleus of an atom could be enlarged to the size of a sesame seed. If that sesame-seed-size nucleus were in the center of a football field, the electrons would be traveling around it at the end of the field. If the proton of a hydrogen atom were the size of a grapefruit, an electron would be zipping around it five miles away!

You can imagine then how much of an atom is matter and how much is empty space. All matter on earth is made of unimaginably small atoms with even smaller parts, some moving at incredible speeds, all in relative emptiness. Only the Creator of this invisible world understands how it all comes together and holds together to make up gold and rain and oak trees and your little finger.

"All things were made by him; and without him was not any thing made that was made."   *John 1:3*

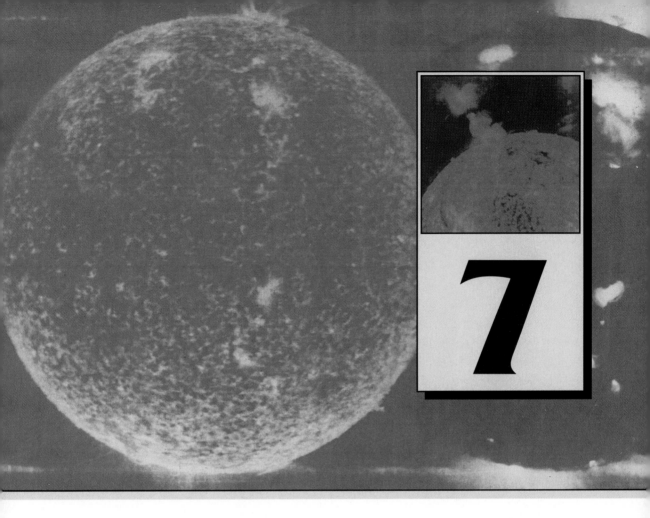

The Sun

"From the rising of the sun unto the going down of the same the Lord's name is to be praised." Psalm 113:3

The sun warms us, measures our time, and provides us with light. It has always dominated our sky, our scientific study, and our very existence. It is, as the astronomer Copernicus said, the governor of earth. It makes life possible on our planet. What do you think would happen if the sun went dark, even for a month?

The sun is a star, but just an average one. It is small and rather dim compared to many of the hundreds of billions of other stars in the universe. It is only a speck in our Milky Way galaxy. And our Milky Way is just one of the billions of galaxies that we know of.

To get a glimpse of how big the universe is requires a strong imagination. The fastest thing that we know in the universe is light; it travels at 186,000 miles a second. At that speed a jet could circle the earth seven and a half times in a second. Scientists chose the distance light travels in a year, or the *light-year*, as a standard unit of measure. At 186,000 miles per second, light travels about 6 trillion miles in one year. Suppose we had a spaceship that could travel a billion times the speed of light. We might be able to visit 100 galaxies in one earth day. But even then, it would take more than 250,000 years to see all the galaxies.

From that larger perspective, our sun all but gets lost. But compared to what we are most familiar with—the earth and the moon—the sun is impressive indeed. The dimensions and power of even this small star are almost beyond our comprehension.

The Nature of the Sun

People have always been intrigued with the sun. Some people, such as the ancient Egyptians, worshiped it as a god. Others used it to calculate seasons and to establish calendar days. The Mayans, for example, found a way to adjust their calendar that is more accurate than our practice of adding an extra day every four years. Still other people were fascinated trying to find out how far away the sun was from the earth and whether the earth traveled around the sun or vice versa. It was not until the early 1900s, though, that anyone had the equipment to get detailed pictures of the sun accurately.

Diameter

For a long time, people thought that the sun and the moon both traveled around the earth. And they thought the sun and the moon were equal in size. The sun is 93 million miles from the earth. But the moon is 400 times closer to us–and 400 times smaller. If the sun were 100 feet away, the moon would be about three inches away.

You have probably already learned in math that the diameter of a circle is the distance across its center. How big do you think the sun's diameter is? It is over 865,000 miles–more than 100 times the earth's diameter and more than 400 times the moon's. If you can imagine putting 109 earths side by side, you have some idea of the distance of the sun across its center. The sun is so large that the moon could orbit the earth inside the sun with 94,000 miles to spare.

Volume

Suppose that you had a gigantic tub of water. If you could somehow drop the earth inside the tub and measure the amount of water that splashed out, you could measure the earth's volume. Imagine that you could try the same experiment using the sun. If the sun were solid like the earth, it would splash out one million times as much water as earth because the sun's volume is one million times the earth's volume. In other words, it would take a million earths to fill up as much space as the sun would.

A million earths is hard to imagine. A million of anything is hard to imagine. One million pennies stacked would make a pile almost a mile high. One million seconds equals about twelve days. One million hours adds up to about 114 years.

Because of its size and its color, the sun is called a *yellow dwarf*. Some stars that are brighter and hotter than the sun are blue stars. Red stars are dimmer than our sun. A *white dwarf* is an even dimmer star, about the size of earth. Rarely discernible to the naked eye, the colors of stars are best seen through a telescope.

Although the sun's volume is much greater than the earth's volume, its weight is not. The sun weighs 300,000 times as much as earth. The earth weighs 6,600,000,000,000,000,000,000 (6.6 sextillion) tons. Imagine how much the sun must weigh! Why would a body with one million times the volume of earth weigh only 300,000 times as much? What do you think the sun is mostly made of? It is made of gases. Is the earth made mostly of gases?

Mass

Mass is not the same as weight. Mass refers to how much matter is in an object. Weight can change depending on where you are, but mass is always the same. To measure mass we compare one object with an unknown mass to an object whose mass we know.

It would take 333,000 earths to equal the mass of the sun. The sun alone makes up 98.5 percent of the total mass of the whole solar system. If you could combine all the planets, their moons, the comets, the asteroids, and the dust of the solar system into one huge ball, it would still take 750 of those balls to equal the mass of the sun.

Gravity

You probably remember that gravity is the force that one thing has on another. The earth's gravity holds the moon in orbit and keeps you from floating off into space. Which do you think has the greater pull of gravity–the earth or the sun? Which has more mass? The more mass an object has, the greater pull of gravity it has. Since the sun is so massive, its force of gravity is twenty-eight times greater than earth's. If it were possible to survive the intense heat of the sun long enough to get on the scales, how much would a 75-pound earthling weigh on the sun? He would weigh 2,100 pounds. Would he look like he weighed that much? No. His mass would be the same. A man who weighs 165 pounds on earth would weigh 4,610 pounds on the sun. How much would you weigh on the sun?

Structure of the Sun

The Interior of the Sun

Scientists believe the core of the sun is hot, thick gases that make up what might be called the "furnace." The gases here must be at least 20,000,000 degrees Fahrenheit, and perhaps as much as 27,000,000 degrees Fahrenheit. The main gas here is *hydrogen,* the lightest matter we know of. Under the billions of tons of pressure from the outer parts of the sun, hydrogen atoms break apart. Protons of hydrogen come together, or *fuse,* in a new way. They form a different and heavier gas called *helium.* Hydrogen and helium make up about 98 percent of the sun's matter.

When hydrogen is crushed and split and some of its protons recombine, other protons become neutrons. When they do, a tiny bit of their matter changes into

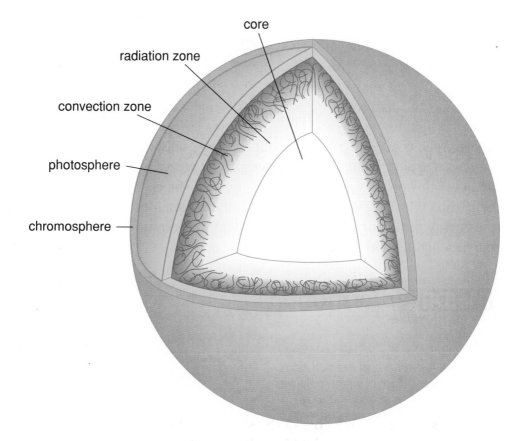

core

radiation zone

convection zone

photosphere

chromosphere

light and heat energy. This change is called *nuclear fusion*. Nuclear fusion can continue until the star runs out of hydrogen. The released energy—*wave energy*—travels outward through the sun until it reaches the sun's surface. At the same time, fusion causes another kind of energy called *particle energy*. Particles are tiny bits of matter, so small that some of them cannot be seen even under a microscope. Particle energy moves outward, too, but not as fast as wave energy does.

The nuclear fusion in the core of the sun is constantly radiating energy outward. From the core the solar energy is absorbed into the radiation zone, the sun's largest layer. The solar energy, now in the form of waves, then passes outward, away from the core of the sun. In the *convective zone* the energy meets atoms that can absorb great amounts of power. The energy superheats the convective cells, sending tremendous heat and light to the surface. Once the gases have released the heat and light, they cool and sink, only to be turned again in the mighty furnaces of the core. Over and over this process goes on, making the sun shine. Our whole planet is warmed by a mere one billionth of the energy the sun sends forth. Where does the rest of the heat and light go?

INSIDE Information

Particle energy and wave energy heat the surface of the sun as a fire heats a pot of water–only with trillions of times more energy. When convective cells become superheated, they rise, bursting and bubbling, to the surface. From earth the rising convective cells look like grains of rice boiling up. Scientists think that they are the heads of giant columns of gas that are rising up from inside the sun. They each last only about five to eight minutes, and new ones are always forming. Some of these cells are larger than the state of Texas; others would cover twice the earth's diameter. Their constant activity gives the sun a bubbly, boiling appearance.

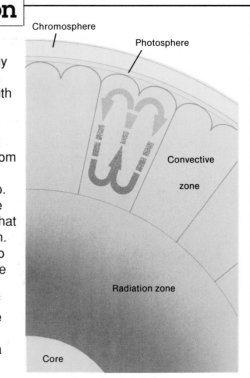

Chromosphere

Photosphere

Convective zone

Radiation zone

Core

The Sun's Atmosphere

When you draw pictures of the sun as a big yellow or orange ball, you are really drawing only one part of the sun–its surface. The surface of the sun is called the *photosphere*. The name means "ball of light." **Never** look directly at the sun either with your naked eye or through a telescope or glasses. Looking directly at the sun can damage your eyes permanently. Telescopes and magnifying glasses only magnify the sun's glare. Although you may not feel pain for a few seconds, the sun can already be injuring your eyes.

The photospheric layer of gases is only about 60 miles thick and has a temperature of about 11,000 degrees Fahrenheit. Besides the bright surface, the sun has a large atmosphere that is divided into two parts. You normally cannot see the atmosphere because the sun's surface is too bright. A solar eclipse–an event that happens when the moon blocks the sun's surface from earth's view–shows the atmosphere.

Scientists can also see the atmosphere using a special instrument called a *coronagraph* that can produce an artificial eclipse of the sun. During a solar eclipse you can see a thin pink layer called the *chromosphere* and then a glowing layer called the *corona*. Which layer do you think means "color sphere"? The chromosphere gets its reddish pink from the glowing hydrogen gases. The chromosphere extends out about 10,000 miles. It may have temperatures from 7,000 to 10,000 degrees Fahrenheit.

The outermost part of the sun is a glowing white halo of gases. Since it looks like a crown for the sun, scientists named it *corona,* the Latin word for "crown." The corona begins at the top of the chromosphere and has no definite outer boundary. It extends in all directions for millions of miles. The corona is never the same shape; it is constantly changing. It shifts and rises in huge, leaping tongues of thin, hot gas.

Perhaps you wonder why with all this nuclear reaction and incredible production of energy going on that the sun does not just blow apart. Since the sun is a body of immense size, it also has strong gravity. Gravity tends to keep the sun pulled in toward itself. Some scientists think that it is the pressure of the sun inward that generates its energy. Also, intense magnetic fields band the corona, pressing and contorting it.

Special Features

Spicules

Huge jets of flame shoot up from the chromosphere and extend thousands of miles into the sun's corona. These fiery points are called *spicules*, after the Latin word for "spike." The average diameter of each spicule is about 500 miles, and it may shoot out at a speed of 20 miles a second. At times these jets of flame seem to stand still minutes before they fade away or fall like a collapsing tower. To some people, the spiky tops of the spicules resemble wheat fields blowing in the wind. Others think they look like blades of burning grass. What do they look like to you?

Solar Wind

The temperature of the corona can rise as high as 1 to 2 million degrees Fahrenheit. At this high temperature particles from the corona boil away from the sun, taking part of the sun's magnetic field. These particles travel through space as the *solar wind*. This wind escapes through large holes in the corona and travels out into the far reaches of the solar system at 200 to 500 miles per second. Which reaches earth first, solar wind or solar light?

How far does the solar wind reach into space? Scientists think that it extends at least twelve times the distance from the earth to the sun. Its maximum distance may be four times as far as Pluto's distance from the sun. Pluto is 3,660 million miles from the sun. How far might solar winds reach?

Look at the drawing of a comet going around the sun. In which direction does the comet's tail point? Wherever the comet travels in its orbit, its head always points toward the sun and the tail always streams off in the opposite direction. Can you explain why? Scientists used to think that the pressure of the sunlight pushed the tail away. They have since learned that this pressure is not strong enough to force the comet's gases away from its head. They now know that a stream of particles from the solar wind blows the tail away from the sun.

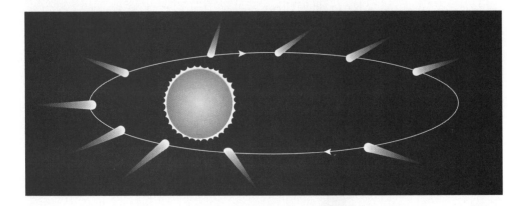

Sunspots

When scientists look at the sun through telescopes, they see dark areas called *sunspots*. Galileo discovered them in 1610 and observed that over a period of several days the spots seem to move from east to west across the sun's surface. Actually, they do not move at all but appear to move because the sun rotates, about once every twenty-seven days. The sun, however, does not rotate at the same speed in all places. It seems to rotate faster at its equator than at its poles. Why do you suppose this is so?

The sunspots are areas of magnetic activity on the sun. These areas of magnetism affect the heating process and produce cool spots. These cooler areas– about 3,600 degrees Fahrenheit–soon turn a darker color. The sunspots may range from a few thousand miles to a hundred thousand miles. The largest sunspot on record is 12,000 times greater than the surface of earth. How long sunspots last before disintegrating depends on their size. The largest spots last longer than the smaller ones. Small sunspots may last one or two days, but the large ones may last several weeks. One sunspot lasted eighteen months. The number of sunspots rise and fall in what is known as a sunspot cycle. About every eleven years the number of sunspots reaches its highest number.

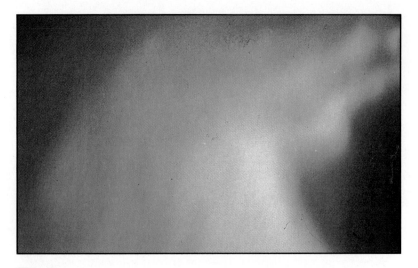

Flares

When sunspots appear, often another unusual event occurs called a flare. *Flares* are sudden explosions of energy that shoot out great light and heat. Most scientists think that they are caused by magnetic storms in the chromosphere. Although the sun looks no brighter to earth during a solar flare, the extra energy does occasionally affect our atmosphere.

A few days after a solar flare, some particles thrown out by the flare become trapped in the earth's magnetic field. At the North and South poles, where the magnetic field is usually the weakest, the particles fall deeper into the atmosphere, coming closer to earth's surface. As they do, they generate electric currents, sending shimmering sheets of light through our skies. We call these dazzling curtains of light the *aurora borealis* (northern lights) and the *aurora australis* (southern lights). Have you ever seen an aurora?

Flares can also send out enough particles to cause magnetic storms on earth. The bombardment of solar particles increases the earth's magnetic field and disrupts radio communication. Once, several solar flares appeared in a few days, and the magnetic storm that resulted blew up a large transformer in Canada.

Prominences

One of the most graceful and beautiful occurrences on the chromosphere is the *prominences*. Often looking like brilliant trees or flaming fishtails, prominences are great loops of hot gas. These streams of erupting hydrogen stretch far into the sun's corona. They are not as violent as flares. Sometimes they rise up in a sweeping arch larger than our earth and then fall in an hour. Sometimes they stand out from the sun for more than a week. Frequently, prominences blow completely away from the sun.

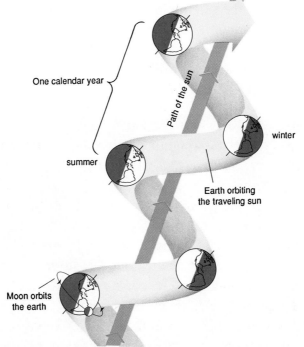

One calendar year

Path of the sun

summer

winter

Earth orbiting the traveling sun

Moon orbits the earth

The Traveling Sun

Everything in the solar system that you have studied so far is moving. Both the earth and the moon rotate. The moon orbits the earth and the earth orbits the sun. What do you predict about the sun? It rotates. Does it revolve also? If it does, in what direction is it moving? And how fast is it moving?

127

The Milky Way galaxy is an immense spiral of stars, 100,000 light-years across, with a concentration of stars in the middle. The sun is moving around the center of this galaxy about 175 miles per second. It is held in space by the gravitational pull of the other stars, which each have their own orbits. In this way the Milky Way is like a huge solar system: the stars, like giant planets, orbit the center of the galaxy. Our galaxy is also moving. It is rotating like a giant pinwheel in space. All its stars rotate with it.

Despite the vastness of the universe and the stars that are more than the sand in all our oceans, God makes special mention of our sun. He declared it the ruler of our daytime on the fourth day of creation. He put the sun in the heavens for our good, to ''give light upon the earth'' (Genesis 1:17).

''And God made two great lights; the greater light to rule the day, and the lesser light to rule the night: he made the stars also.''   *Genesis 1:16*

Finding Out . . .

About the Sun's Diameter

1. Locate a sidewalk or large yard where you can walk in a long straight line without interruption and three wooden stakes or a piece of chalk. Or get 109 Cheerios, a pencil, a large sheet of brown paper, and two yards of string.

2. Mark the spot where you begin with a stake or chalk mark and put your heel against the mark. Place a mark in front of your toe. Now walk 108 more steps from that point, putting one foot directly in front of the other. Mark where you stop.

3. Lay 109 Cheerios in a row on the large piece of paper. Tie one end of the string around the pencil. Hold the other end on the fifty-fifth Cheerio so that the pencil point touches the outside of the last Cheerio. Have a partner draw a circle on the paper with the pencil.

4. Compare the model of the sun to the model of the earth.

Finding Out . . .

About the Sun's Power

1. Get a solar cell, a compass, fine insulated wire, a shoe box, tape or glue, and a magnifying mirror.

2. Wrap the compass neatly with the wire several times. Connect the ends of the wire to the solar cell terminals or wires.

3. Tape or glue the solar cell to the shoe box for support. Lay the compass so that the needle is under the coils of wire.

4. Shade the solar cell with your hand. Then let the sunlight hit the cell. What happens to the needle? What do you think will happen when you use the magnifying mirror to reflect light onto the cell? Turn the mirror until it directs a small, bright patch of light onto the cell. What happens to the needle? Why do you think the mirror makes the needle move differently? Record your observations.

8 Heat

"But the day of the Lord will come as a thief in the night; in the which the heavens shall pass away with a great noise, and the elements shall melt with fervent heat, the earth also and the works that are therein shall be burned up."   *II Peter 3:10*

What Is Heat?

Why does ice cream melt? To find out, you must investigate a kind of energy called *heat*. You may be surprised to learn that heat is not really the hotness or coldness of something. Rather, it is the reason that things are hot or cold, warm or cool.

The smallest child knows something about hot and cold, although he could not say what heat is exactly. He can recognize that his food cools off if he dawdles too long in eating it. He quickly learns that a stove is often painfully hot. Scientists are in much the same position. Not one scientist can say he truly knows how heat is produced. To help themselves understand what they see heat do, scientists make up theories about where heat comes from.

Energy is defined as the ability to do work. This ability has many forms. Light is energy, and so is electricity. There are also nuclear and chemical energies. Energy can change from one form into another. For example, in a flashlight battery the chemical energy of the batteries is changed to electrical energy. In the bulb, the electrical energy becomes light and heat energy.

As you studied earlier, we believe all matter is made up of atoms, the tiny building blocks of the universe. These small particles are always moving. Sometimes they move fast, sometimes not so fast. The movement, fast or slow, produces energy. Which do you think makes more energy–fast or slow movement? Energy of movement is called *kinetic* energy. What do you think the Greek word means from which we get *kinetic?*

Most scientists think that when molecules move, some of the kinetic energy changes into heat energy and some is stored as potential energy in the atoms that make up the molecules. Heat is the total of the kinetic and stored energy in matter. The faster the molecules move, the more heat energy is given off. What do you think accounts for coolness in matter?

When something feels cool to you, its molecules are not moving as fast as the molecules in your hand are. Your hand is warmer than the thing it touches. What can you say about something hot?

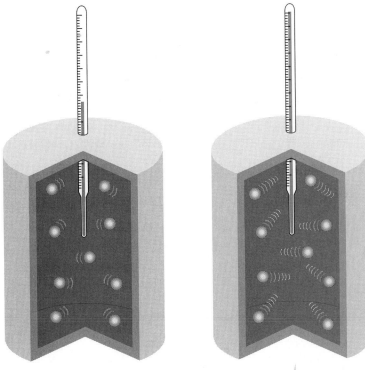

Finding Out . . .

About Changing Energy Forms

1. Get two paper cups, some dry sand, a bulb thermometer, some adhesive tape, a pencil, and your notebook.

2. Pour some sand into one of the cups. Put the thermometer into the sand and record the temperature. Then put the other cup upside down on the first cup and seal the cups together with tape. Shake the sand vigorously for at least five minutes.

3. Punch a hole in the bottom of one cup with the pencil. Put the thermometer into the sand through the hole. What is the temperature of the sand now? Do you think the temperature would be higher if you had shaken the sand longer?

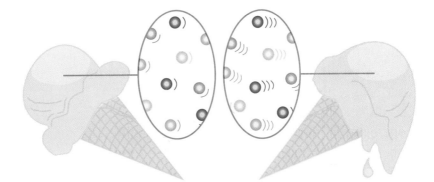

What Heat Does

Since energy is the ability to do work, heat can do work. Heat can change the way things look. Heat can make water turn to steam, for example. But heat does not change the composition of water when it turns it to steam. Steam and water are made of the same amounts and combination of oxygen and hydrogen atoms.

Now, think again about melting ice cream. When you buy an ice cream cone, the ice cream is hard because it has just come out of the cold freezer. How do you think the molecules are moving in the ice cream? Why are they moving slowly? Then you take the cone in your hand and walk outside. If it is a hot summer day, you have to start licking the ice cream right away, don't you? If it is a crisp fall day, you may have a little longer to begin eating. But the ice cream will start to melt eventually. Why?

The molecules in your hand and in the air are moving faster than the molecules in the ice cream because your hand and the air are warmer. The molecules in the air collide with the molecules in the ice cream. Those ice cream molecules begin to move faster, being bumped by the faster molecules around them. What happens when the ice cream molecules move faster? Their kinetic energy becomes heat energy. As the molecules speed up, they use more space. Why do you think the ice cream melts on the outside first?

The heat energy in the ice cream begins to change the state of the ice cream. It changes the ice cream from a solid to a liquid, just as it turned water into steam. Did the heat change the composition of the ice cream? When you lick the melted ice cream from the side of the cone or from your hand, does it taste any different from the ice cream that has not melted? No. Liquid or solid, the ingredients of ice cream are the same.

What work did heat do in the case of the ice cream? It caused the molecules in the ice cream to move faster, and it caused the ice cream to change states. How do you think putting melted ice cream into the freezer makes the ice cream go back to a solid state? When you first put the ice cream into the freezer, it is warmer than the air around it. What can you say about its molecules right then?

The faster-moving ice cream molecules may cause the air molecules near it to speed up a little. But they do not have enough energy to get enough air molecules moving to heat up the freezer. By and by, the ice cream molecules release their heat energy and slow down. What happens to the ice cream then?

What Heat Does to Liquids and Gases

1. Get a small empty metal juice can, a little dish-washing liquid, a washcloth, some water, some food coloring, some modeling clay, a plastic straw, a pan, a teaspoon, a narrow-necked pint jar or bottle, a felt-tip pen, and a hot plate (or be able to use a stove).

2. Mix a teaspoon of dish-washing liquid with five teaspoons of water. Dip the open end of the juice can into the diluted dish-washing liquid. Set the can upright, and wrap your hands tightly around it. What happens to the bubble? Wet the washcloth in very cold water. Wrap the cloth around the can. Observe what happens.

3. Fill the pint bottle with water and mix in some food coloring. Mold some clay around the middle of the straw, and then put the straw into the bottle, making a tight seal on the bottle with the clay. What happens to the water in the straw? Mark the water level on the straw. Set the bottle in the pan and set the pan on the burner. Heat the pan and the water. What do you observe? Mark the new water level. Let the water cool. What happens?

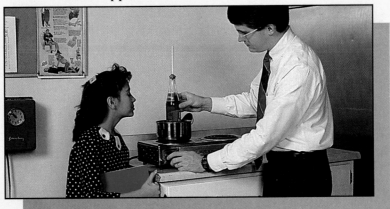

How Heat Travels

Heat does not stay in one place. If it did, your furnace or air conditioner would not have to come on several times a day. You would not need a blanket at night, and you could sell your refrigerator.

You have already seen one way heat travels. When faster-moving molecules bump into slower molecules and start them moving–as in the melting ice cream–heat travels by *conduction*. When heat passes from molecule to molecule, the heat moves but the molecules stay in nearly the same place. You might think of conduction as dominoes falling down in a line, the dominoes representing molecules and the force knocking them over representing heat. Have you ever held a metal spoon in iced tea or hot chocolate? What happened to the spoon? It changed temperature by conduction.

Another way heat travels is *convection*. In convection, heat does not move through a molecule but rather moves with a molecule. You studied an important result of convection when you studied winds. Do you remember that warm air rises because it is lighter than cool air? And that when cool air takes the place of the rising warm air, a breeze or wind develops? The trade winds and sea breezes are examples of convection because the heat and the air move together.

Convection means that when a certain amount of a liquid or gas is heated, the heated liquid or gas moves–not just the heat, as in conduction. When you heat a pan

of water on the stove, you can see swirls in the water just before it boils. Those swirls are convection currents. All the water that is most heated rises at the same time. What happens to the cooler water? How does all the water in the pan eventually get hot?

If you did the *Finding Out* activity about storms in the chapter on weather, you saw convection working as the dark food coloring moved in the warming water. Do you think ocean currents develop by conduction or convection?

One other way that heat travels is by *radiation.* When matter–solid, liquid, or gas–is not involved in getting heat from one place to another, we say the energy is radiated. The way the sun heats the earth is the best example of radiation. The heat travels from the sun through space and warms the earth. Do you think ice cream left in direct sunlight will melt more because of conduction or radiation? When you put your hands out to the fireplace, are you warmed more by conduction or radiation?

Finding Out . . .

How Heat Travels

1. Get a beaker or a glass, a teaspoon of cornstarch, tincture of iodine, a medicine dropper, a metal pie pan, a candle, a match, a bulb thermometer, and some water.

2. Fill the beaker two-thirds full with water and stir in the cornstarch. Put the beaker in the pie pan. When the water becomes still, put in one drop of tincture of iodine. What happens to the water? What effect does the tincture have on cornstarch? Light the candle and hold it near the bottom of the glass, not letting the flame touch the glass. Watch the top and sides of the cornstarch.

3. Keep the flame by the glass for a few minutes. Then blow out the candle and measure the temperature of the water at the top of the glass. Then measure the temperature of the water at the bottom of the glass. Do not stir the water as you do the measurements. Which part of the water was heated by convection? Which by conduction? Was radiation involved at all?

When a material lets heat pass through easily, we say the material is a good *conductor*. If it does not let heat pass through easily, we call the material an *insulator*. Air is a good insulator. Birds fluff out their feathers on cold days. The air between their feathers and their bodies makes good insulation. Why do you think it is a good idea to wear several layers of clothing in cold weather?

Some solids are good insulators. Have you ever noticed that metal pans in your kitchen usually have wooden or hard plastic handles? Why do you think they have such handles instead of metal ones? Metals conduct heat well. Glass, hard plastic, and wood do not. Why do you have to use pot holders on some pans?

Perhaps you have heard someone say that he was putting insulation in his house. Why do you think he wanted to do that? Suppose he puts the insulation in the floor of his attic. What will happen in the winter when the warm air rises in his house? The insulation will keep the heat from going out through the roof. How will the insulation help in the summer?

Finding Out . . .

About Insulation

1. Ask at a hardware store or a building supply company for some scraps of different kinds of insulating materials. Get five glass jars with lids, five bulb thermometers, some rubber bands, some newspaper, a piece of wool, and some hot water.

2. Wrap one jar in newspaper and secure the paper with rubber bands. Wrap one jar loosely in wool. Wrap the others with the different kinds of insulation and secure with rubber bands. Pour the same amount of water into each jar. Measure and record the temperature of the water (do not let the thermometer bulb touch the jar). Put on the lids, and cover each lid with the same material the jar is wrapped in.

3. Feel the outside of the insulation. Did much heat come through? Take the insulation off and feel the inside of it. Measure and record the temperature of the water. Repeat this procedure for each of the insulation materials you have.

4. Decide which insulation works best to keep heat from escaping. Can you say how the insulation pieces reduce the flow of heat?

Talking About Heat

When you talk about heat, you probably use words such as "warm," "cool," "very hot," and "cold." These terms may be meaningful to your friends, but are they exact enough for cooking or conducting experiments? What you think is warm, another person may think is hot. A more consistent method is necessary if we are to make any definite statements about heat.

Heat is sometimes called *thermal energy. Therme* is the Greek word for "heat." What do you think *thermometer* literally means? It means "heat meter." How is a thermometer better than our skin in telling the air temperature? If your hands are cold from making snowballs, the warm air in your house may feel much warmer than it really is.

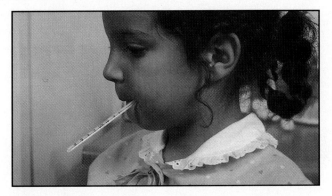

Can you think of times when it is especially important to record temperatures? How about for patients in the hospital? Doctors watch carefully whether a person's body temperature rises or falls. They can tell by the change in temperature how the person is responding to medicine or treatment.

Weather forecasters pay strict attention to air temperatures. By looking over records from previous years, they can predict the average temperature for a certain coming month. Changes in air temperature during the day can signal approaching storms as well.

You are probably familiar with the most common kind of thermometer. It is a glass tube with red alcohol or silver mercury in it. The space above the liquid is mostly a vacuum. If the bulb is in a warm place, the molecules in the liquid begin to vibrate. As they do, they take up more space, and the liquid expands. What happens to the liquid? If the bulb is in a cool place, heat will travel from the bulb to the cooler matter. The molecules in the liquid slow down. What happens to the liquid then?

INSIDE Information

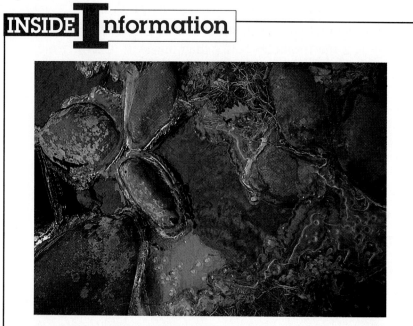

Almost every kind of matter we know of *expands* when heated and *contracts* when cooled. But there is one important exception to this rule: water.

God made water so that when it gets near its freezing point, it stops contracting and starts to expand. As it freezes, it expands even more. As you know, things that expand are lighter. Ice, therefore, floats. If water did not have this special quality, water in ponds would probably freeze from the bottom up. What would happen to the living things then? God provided for their safety by making water the exception to the rules of heating and cooling.

The amount of movement of the liquid up and down in the thermometer is a measure of the kinetic energy in the liquid. We call this measure *temperature*. To be able to say it is forty degrees outside is a much better description than to say it is chilly.

But we must be sure to say forty degrees on what scale. The two scales most often used are the *Fahrenheit* and the *Celsius* scales. Both these scales are based on the boiling and freezing points of water. On the Fahrenheit scale, the freezing point is 32 degrees; on the Celsius scale it is 0 degrees. The boiling point is 212 degrees on the Fahrenheit and 100 on the Celsius. All scientists use the Celsius scale. Why do you think it is helpful for scientists all over the world to use the same scale?

Perhaps you have heard someone talking about "burning up calories." A *calorie* is a measure of how much energy is used in doing certain things. One calorie is how much energy it takes to raise the temperature of one gram of water one degree Celsius. How much energy do two calories represent?

Finding Out . . .

About Recording Temperature

1. Get an empty aluminum can, a glass cake pan, two thermometers, a large beaker, hot water, cool water, and your notebook.

2. Pour 250 milliliters of hot water into the can. Put the can into the cake pan, and pour 500 milliliters of cool water into the pan. Using two thermometers, measure the temperature of the water in both containers. Repeat every thirty seconds for ten minutes, stirring the water briefly before each measurement.

3. Mark your measurements on the graph each time. What does your record show about movement of heat?

The Nervous System

How do you find out about anything? How do you know about your friend, for instance? You listen to him talk, you see him, you shake his hand or pat his shoulder, you may even recognize a particular scent he usually has. You know him by your senses. Nearly everyone can name five senses: seeing, hearing, tasting, smelling, touching. But scientists have recently found more than fifteen other sense systems. One such system seems to register the length of days and helps your body adjust to changes in season.

All the information that comes to your senses is sent to your brain in a complicated and wonderfully designed network called your *nervous system*. It is a system that makes all the telephone networks in the world seem like little more than poorly made toys. It is the means by which you come to know and interpret everything in your world.

Parts and Functions of the Nervous System

How do you know when you prick your finger on a pin? Because it hurts? Yes, but how do you know it hurts? The answer to that question involves some amazing facts.

All over your body in layers of your skin and inside your body on organs and muscles are sensitive cells called *neurons*. Many look somewhat like microscopic trees. When the point of a pin pushes against one of the fine branches on one of these ''trees,'' the sensation of the pinpoint travels through the branch to the main body of the cell. Then the feeling moves into the ''trunk'' and ''roots.''

Between the ''roots'' of one neuron and the ''branches'' of the next is a small space. The sensation from the pin cannot jump across the space. However, chemicals released at the end of the neuron cause the next neuron to carry the message on. And so the information from the tip of your finger zips along–at more than 300 feet per second.

You have billions of neurons in your body, but they are not evenly spaced throughout. Which do you think has more neurons per square inch–your fingers or your back? Which do you depend on more for finding out by touch? Your fingers. Your fingertips have more than 9,000 nerve endings per inch on their surfaces.

When a sensation such as a prick or a burn reaches the main line to the brain, the *spinal cord,* two things happen. The first is that an automatic message is sent back to your finger (or whatever place felt the prick or burn), telling your muscles to jerk the finger away. This response does not wait for your brain to make the decision; it is called a *reflex.*

The other thing that happens is that messages are sent to your brain. The brain interprets them and you know that you pricked or burned your finger and pulled it away. Do you think that you feel the pain or respond to it first? It may seem that everything happens at once. But you actually pull your hand back before your brain tells you there is pain. Since the whole process is incredibly fast, you do not notice the time difference. From the time the pin touched your skin until you jerked your finger away and your brain registered what has happened was less than one-thousandth of a second.

Some messages from the neurons do not require reflex action. Such messages go to the brain and get interpreted. The brain then sends messages out as needed. For example, when you sit in one position for a long time, neurons send a message of discomfort to the brain. The brain receives and interprets the messages and sends messages to the muscles of your legs, causing you to change the way you are sitting.

Imagine that you were given a computer that could hold a lifetime of information without ever changing disks, that could sort and hold data from a million sources at one time, that could make up stories and recall tunes, that could register and regulate temperature, wake you up in the morning, alert you to danger, and register the slightest change in your environment. And suppose that this phenomenal piece of equipment weighed only about three pounds at its largest and was easily carried. Such a computer is still far beyond the reach of science and technology. But you have such a gift right now–your brain.

The human brain is more complex and more wonderful than its own imagination can even consider. Beside it, the fastest computers are slow and inefficient. Compared to it, the best communication system in the world is little better than the pony express. Most of the brain's work is a puzzle to scientists. They know what the brain looks like, what its parts are, and what it does for us. But they do not know *how* it does all it does.

For a long time, people thought that the brain was like a bowl of water with dikes and canals in it. Later, doctors and other scientists discovered that the brain is made of *gray matter,* a special material packed with neurons and fed by many blood vessels. How would you describe the appearance of the gray matter? Why do you think it is "wrinkled"? The folds and dips allow more of this special material to fit into the skull. Although much of the brain looks like one mass, it really has many specialized areas. Different parts of the brain do different things.

The front of the brain is called the *frontal lobes.* When you run or do a pull-up or move in any conscious way, the directions come from this part of your brain. When you are awake, these lobes are in control, making you alert to what is going on around you, causing you to have the personality you have. Here you reason, plan, make decisions. The frontal lobes make it possible for you to memorize information and to talk.

Just behind and below the frontal lobes are the *temporal lobes.* Here sounds are interpreted and

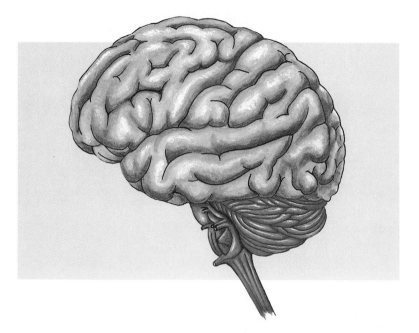

remembered. Some tastes are registered here. This part of your brain helps you remember tunes, the sounds of words, and certain sights.

Behind the frontal lobes are the *parietal lobes,* the centers for interpreting pain, touch, temperature, some tastes, and pressure. If you were holding a cat in your lap, the parietal lobes would send messages to the frontal lobes about the warmth and the weight of the cat on your legs, the softness of the cat's fur, and–if the cat worked its claws into your thigh–pain. What part of the brain would tell you that the cat was purring?

At the back of the brain are the *occipital lobes.* These lobes receive messages from the eyes, interpret them, and store information about what you see. What other part of the brain also stores some memories of what you have seen? Have you ever hit your head and seen ''stars''? What part of your brain was probably jarred?

All these lobes of the brain together are called the *cerebrum.* The name comes from the Latin word for ''brain.'' The cerebrum takes up most of the space in your skull, but it is not all of your brain.

Under the occipital lobes is the *cerebellum*. This part of the brain is somewhat like a dispatcher. It receives orders from the frontal lobes and sends messages to muscles throughout the body to accomplish the orders. The cerebellum does not decide when or where you should move, but it does control the speed and force with which you move. If you want to pick up a banana, your cerebellum controls your arm and hand so that you do not snatch the fruit and squash it. Have you ever picked up something that was not as heavy as it looked? What happened? You probably lifted the object too high and too fast. Your brain had miscalculated the force that was needed.

The *brain stem* is the part that controls some functions of your body that you hardly ever think about: breathing, heartbeat, blood pressure, and swallowing. These activities go on whether or not you think about them; they are *involuntary* activities. Why do you think God designed our brains to operate some functions automatically? Could you read this paragraph and remember to pump your blood and breathe at the same time? Could you go to sleep?

The brain stem leads right into the spinal cord, the strands of nerves from the brain that go down your back inside your backbone. The backbone protects this main link between your brain and all other parts of your body. Nerves branch out from the spinal cord and keep branching so that even the smallest toe has a communication route with the brain. Despite all distances, from the moment you decide to do something until your brain alerts the proper muscles and the job is done is a phenomenally short time. Just how short often depends on how tired you are or how hard you are concentrating.

Finding Out . . .

About Reaction Time

1. Get a meter stick, a pencil, and your notebook.

2. Hold the meter stick by the 100-cm end. Have your science partner hold his thumb and forefinger around the 50-cm mark without touching the meter stick. Without saying when you will do it, drop the meter stick. Your partner should try to catch the stick as soon as he can. Record the number where your partner caught the stick. Do the experiment three times, recording the number each time. Then trade jobs, with your partner holding the stick and you catching it.

3. Fill out the notebook page and the graph. How did your reaction time compare to your partner's? What parts of your brain helped you with this activity?

Other Functions of the Brain

Sleep

When you go to sleep, you go into a state of *unconsciousness*. That is, your frontal lobes are not receiving or interpreting messages from your nerves. But your brain is still active. What parts in particular must keep sending out messages? As we first "drift off," the brain is not very active at all. Then we enter the first stage, a light sleep. In a little while, we go into a deep sleep. Later the brain becomes active, and the eyes move quickly back and forth, back and forth, as if we might be watching a tennis match on fast forward. This is a period of sleep that researchers call *rapid eye movement,* or REM. Babies spend almost half their sleep in REM. As we grow older, we spend less and less time in REM. REM periods occur about every ninety minutes through the night, lasting from ten minutes to more than half an hour.

INSIDE Information

Did you have a dream last night? Doubtless you did, but you may or may not remember that you did. No one knows for sure why we dream. Some scientists think that we dream in order to file away information, to filter out perceptions we do not need, and even to work out problems we could not solve amid the distractions of waking hours. There may be something to the old saying, "Sleep on it."

Dreams seem to happen during REM. When people are awakened during REM, they nearly always report that they were dreaming. We remember only the few seconds of a dream that go on as we wake up, even though the dream may have been half an hour long.

Sleep is important for mental and physical health. During the time you are awake the brain is busy sending and receiving millions of messages. When you sleep, the brain can work more on other functions such as repairing cuts and bruises or knitting up a broken bone. When you are young, sleep also gives your body time to grow.

The brain stem seems to control sleeping and dreaming. But although other parts of the brain are not as active as during waking hours, they are far from inactive. Your brain filters sounds, for instance, ignoring unimportant or familiar noises while alerting you to sounds that could mean danger or some other disturbance. Have you ever visited someone whose house was near heavy traffic or a railroad? You may have awaked to horns or whistles in the night, but your friend, being used to the sounds, slept through. Why do you think he could sleep?

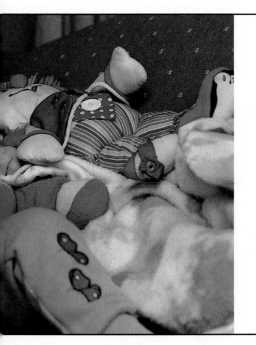

Many people believe that dreams have meaning and should be interpreted. Only on a few occasions has God used dreams to speak to His people. Joseph, for example, was told in a dream to take Mary and the Christ Child to Egypt. Some Christian doctors think that most dreams are a kind of clearinghouse for harmful or unwanted thoughts collected during the time we are awake. The doctors who hold this theory think that trying to remember dreams only causes us to have to dream them over. In any case, dreaming is normal and probably useful–although the whole process remains a mystery.

Memory and Learning

Memory seems to be the one function of the brain that does not operate well during sleep. The brain may be too busy filing away all that happened while you were awake to record what happens while you sleep. It does appear to be true, however, that what you memorize right before you go to sleep you can remember better than if you spent the same amount of time memorizing it some other time.

There are at least three kinds of memory. The shortest is *immediate memory*. It lasts only a few seconds. As you ride a bus, for example, you see many sights out of the window. Your eye sends information to your brain which, for a second or two, holds that information. If the information is not important, if it is not pleasing or painful enough to make an impression, it passes out of our minds.

Other memories are stored for several minutes or hours in *short-term memory*. When you look up a telephone number, for example, your short-term memory holds the number until you use it and sometimes for a little longer. Can you think of other times you use your short-term memory? The more often you repeat looking at or hearing something, the stronger the impression it makes in your brain. Why do you think God commands us to keep our thoughts pure?

Long-term memory lasts for days or for a lifetime. No one knows for sure what causes some memories to be transferred to the long-term files. Many believe that emotions play a big part in the decision. If something is very unpleasant, you want to remember to avoid it. If something is rewarding or comfortable, you want to repeat it. Strong emotions seem to trigger chemical changes in the brain that cause memories to become long-term. Do you think that memorizing a part in a play uses short-term or long-term memory or both?

158

Why do you think it is easier for you to learn subjects that you like than ones in which you have no interest? Perhaps it is partly because you have stronger feelings about some subjects. When your emotions are stirred, your heart beats faster, your blood pressure goes up, and your brain receives more blood. Your memory equipment also goes into a higher gear.

No one has been able to discover exactly how we learn anything. Some scientists think that when you learn something, the outside membrane of a neuron changes. There may be chemical changes inside the neuron also.

Researchers have identified *where* some kinds of learning take place. The cerebrum is divided into halves, a right and a left, joined in the middle by a bundle of more than 200 million nerve fibers. Although the halves may at first seem to be exactly alike, they do look different, and they function separately.

The left side of the cerebrum controls our learning to read, to speak, to do math problems, to perform science experiments. The right side seems to control our ability to compose music, draw pictures, to recognize faces. It also gives you the ability to add tones and emotion to your speech. Most people tend to favor one side of their brains over the other, which means they are more able to do right-brain or left-brain functions.

Some of our ability to learn changes as we grow older. Young children, for example, can learn several languages at once–without getting them mixed together or favoring one over the others. Adults do not learn new languages as easily. But skills such as drawing or playing music can be learned anytime. A famous American artist did not begin to paint until she was seventy-eight years old. And she was still painting when she was 100. Her name was Grandma Moses.

Finding Out . . .

About Memory

1. Get your notebook, a pencil, a stopwatch or a watch with a second hand, and a handout from your teacher.

2. Give your science partner List A that your teacher gave you. For three minutes, let him memorize the list in order. Then let him write on his notebook page as much of the list as he can in one minute. Be sure to time your partner accurately. Do List B and List C in the same way.

3. Trade jobs with your partner, using the lists he gives you. Make sure the times are the same. Fill in your notebook page. You and your science partner should tally your score for each list. Give the lists and your notebook pages to your teacher.

4. The next day, without looking at the lists again, fill in as much of the other notebook page as you can. Get the lists and your other notebook page from your teacher. Tally your scores. How do your scores now compare with the earlier ones? What do you conclude about long-term and short-term memory? Why do you think you remembered some things longer than others?

"A merry heart doeth good like a medicine: but a broken spirit drieth the bones." Proverbs 17:22

Emotions

Emotions can influence far more than our ability to remember. Doctors and scientists now know that worry and fear and anger cause the brain to send out messages such as these: slow down blood flow; release fat into the blood; sweat; vomit; produce more stomach acid. For short periods, these responses can be useful, getting your body ready to run for safety or to fight. But constant worry and fear and anger cause too much fat to be in the blood, the stomach to have too much acid, and so on. By and by, the heart is damaged, the stomach gets ulcers, and the body gets sick easily.

On the other hand, researchers have found that laughter and contentment and hope cause the brain to send commands like these: produce cells that fight disease; lower blood pressure; breathe easier. Can you see God's wisdom in giving us so many instructions about what to do with our problems and how to control our emotions? Scientists have learned that there is as much stress in thinking about a danger as there is in actually seeing a car speeding toward us. To worry then is to face dangers that have not appeared. How much better it is to take your concerns to God and leave them with Him.

"Casting all your care upon him; for he careth for you." I Peter 5:7

The Mind

It is helpful, when studying the nervous system, to read about different parts of the system as though they were completely separate from each other. But really, every part of the brain and the rest of the nervous system are all so interconnected that a change in any part effects all the rest.

For instance, not all the sights you have ever seen are recorded in the same place in your brain. Not all long-term memories are in the same place. Not all the same kinds of learning go on in the same places, although some areas are more important than others. Some smells are remembered in the same place that certain long-term memories are kept. That is the reason that when you smell crayons you may immediately think of your first-grade classroom. Can you think about a scent you like to the point that you actually think you smell it? Many people can because the sense of smell is so closely linked to memory.

Your senses do not function entirely separate from one another either. Have you ever had trouble understanding someone because you could not see his mouth? Have you ever thought food was tasteless when your nose was stuffed up because you had a cold? Both of these cases show how the brain depends on more than one sense at a time to get complete information about something.

The total of all your waking thoughts and your dreams and your actions and speech and behaviors is often referred to as your *mind,* the "you" of *you.* Your will, your personality, your self is more than the sum of the parts of your brain.

God's Word has much to say about how we should use our minds and protect them. Since everything we see, touch, smell, hear, taste, and perceive in any way goes into our brains and since whatever our brains do affects everything about us in turn, we should take care in what we allow to pass into our minds.

We should also be careful to eat and exercise properly. The brain uses about twenty percent of the oxygen and energy that the body produces. When we do not provide well for our bodies or misuse them in any way, the brain and nervous system suffer too. Why is the abuse of drugs against God's will? Our bodies, and especially our brains, are marvelous gifts from our Creator. The more you learn about yourself, the more you will understand the wisdom of the principles God has established for us to live by.

"Finally, brethren, whatsoever things are true, whatsoever things are honest, whatsoever things are just, whatsoever things are pure, whatsoever things are lovely, whatsoever things are of good report; if there be any virtue, and if there be any praise, think on these things."   *Philippians 4:8*

Finding Out . . .

About the Senses

1. Get a piece of apple, cucumber, pear, and banana; a pretzel, a slice of bread, three raisins, some cereal flakes, some toothpicks, a blindfold, and your notebook.

2. Prepare a small bit of five of the foods, putting the fruit and vegetable pieces on toothpicks. Blindfold your partner and ask him to hold his nose closed as you give him bites of food. (He should not have seen the food before.) Ask him to identify the food without seeing or smelling it. Record his guesses.

3. Prepare the foods again in the same way. This time ask your partner to smell the food and then taste it. Ask him to identify each as you give it to him. Record his guesses. Compare his first guesses with his second guesses. What can you conclude about the sense of taste?

10

Plants

"And God said, Let the earth bring forth grass, the herb yielding seed, and the fruit tree yielding fruit after his kind, whose seed is in itself, upon the earth: and it was so. And the earth brought forth grass, and herb yielding seed after his kind, and the tree yielding fruit, whose seed was in itself, after his kind: and God saw that it was good.
                                                    Genesis 1:11-12

When you eat watermelon, do you ever wish that it had fewer seeds? Do you like only seedless grapes? Seeds can be somewhat inconvenient. But without them, many of the plants we enjoy would die out forever.

The process of plants' making more plants is called *reproduction. Reproduce* comes from word parts that mean ''to lead forth again,'' or ''to make again.'' What would have happened if God had not planned for plants to make more plants?

Sexual Reproduction

Sexual reproduction requires cells from two sexes. In most plants the sexes are male and female. The male sex cell is the *sperm;* the female sex cell is the *egg*. (In fungi there are "+" and "−" cells.) The coming together of sex cells is called *fertilization*.

Following fertilization, some plants will produce spores and others will produce seeds. A spore is an organ that forms the "+" and "−" cells. A seed is a little case that contains a tiny plant. Seeds are sometimes in flowers which become fruits, and sometimes they are inside cones.

Reproducing by Spores

Fungi, mosses, and ferns all reproduce by spores. In some kinds of fungi, there are bat-shaped structures underneath the mushroom cap. These structures contain spores. The spores fall from the caps and are carried by the wind to the ground where they will sprout and produce a new fungus plant.

Mosses and liverworts produce structures called *capsules* at the end of stalks following fertilization. The capsules split open and the spores are blown away by the wind. Why do you think it is good that the spores can be blown on the wind? The word *capsule* comes from Latin for "little box." Can you guess why?

If you were to look on the bottom of a fern leaf in summer or fall, you might see small brown dots. Perhaps you have seen them on ferns in flower arrangements from florist shops and thought they were disease spots or insect eggs. The "dots" are actually spore cases that hold hundreds of spores. When the dots dry and split open, the spores pop out. If the ground is moist and shaded, the spores begin to grow. Each spore grows into a small flat plant that is heart-shaped.

This plant does not look like an adult fern. Several weeks later, however, sperm cells and egg cells form. The sperm cells swim to the egg cells, fertilization occurs, and a new plant forms. The new group of cells grows by dividing and producing new cells. Soon it grows leaves and becomes a young fern. The young fern becomes an adult through more growth. Later, it will produce spores on its leaves, and the reproductive cycle begins again.

Finding Out . . .

About Mold Spores

1. Get two slices of bread that has no preservatives, some water, six shallow dishes, six index cards or six labels, and a cover for one dish. You also need a dusty surface and the use of a refrigerator.

2. Rub the bread over a dusty surface to pick up mold spores. Why is it important to prepare all the bread slices alike? Cut the bread slices into thirds. Put one piece into a dish with a table- spoon of water and set it in a refrigerator. Put another piece into a dish with a tablespoon of water and set it in the sunlight. Put another piece into a dish with a tablespoon of water, cover, and set it in a warm, dark place. Put a dry piece into a dish and set it in the refrigerator. Put another dry slice into a dish and set it in the sunlight. The sixth piece you should put into a dish and keep in a dry, cool, lighted place. Assign each dish a separate station number (e.g., Station 1).

3. Check each of the dishes every day for a week or two. Which conditions seem best for growing mold spores?

Reproducing from Seeds in Cones

All conifers sexually reproduce by seeds in cones. Pine trees produce male and female cones. Male cones shed *pollen*. Pollen is a slightly sticky, powdery substance. The sperm cells are inside these pollen grains. *Pollen* comes from a Latin word meaning "flour." Why is this a good name?

Female cones are larger and grow in the upper branches of a pine. The egg cells are formed inside the cones on woody scales. The wind carries the pollen from the male cones to the female cones on other trees.

Why did God create male cones on the bottom of the tree and female cones on the top? The wind blows the pollen between the woody scales of the slightly opened female cones where the egg cells are located. After the pollen enters, the woody scales close. The pollen grains germinate, sending forth narrow pollen tubes that grow toward the egg cells. The tubes grow toward the egg cells and after one year reach the egg cells where fertilization takes place.

INSIDE **I**nformation

After fertilization the new plant begins to grow, cell by cell. It is surrounded by stored food. This plant with its food is the pine *seed*.

In the fall, when the seeds are ripe and when the weather is dry, the woody scales of the female cone open, and the seeds fall to the ground. Some of the seeds are carried by the wind before they land on the ground. The tiny plant inside the seed begins to grow using the stored food.

A root will break through the outside wall of the seed, grow out of the seed, and begin taking in nutrients for the young plant. After several years the young pine becomes an adult and forms male and female cones.

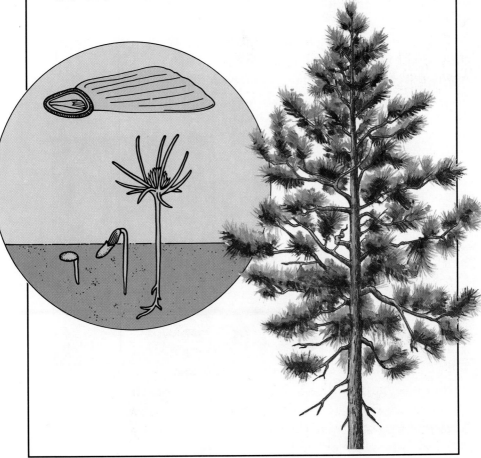

Reproducing from Seeds in Flowers and Fruits

Do you know someone who keeps a flower garden? Do you notice that some plants come back year after year and that others have to be planted new every growing season? The flower is the plant part in which seeds are formed. Flowering plants produce their flowers in different ways. Those that produce their flowers after one growing season and then die are called *annuals*. Most wildflowers are annuals, such as buttercups and red morning glories.

Plants that produce their flowers after two growing seasons and then die are called *biennials*. They have a large main root. Examples are turnips, beets, carrots, and radishes.

Perennials are plants that flower every growing season and live for several years. Woody plants, such as dogwood trees, are perennials. Some wildflowers are perennial, too. One, called meadow beauty, is an herb with pink to purple flowers on tall stems.

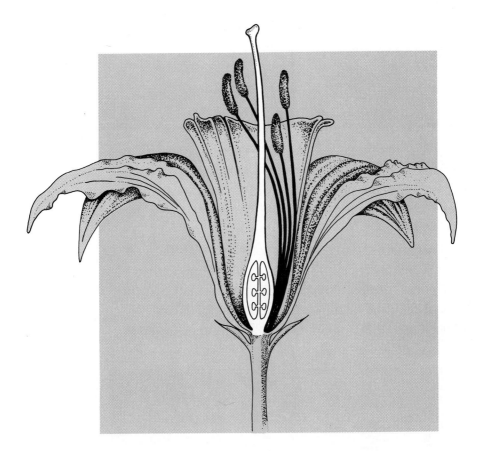

A flower may smell pleasant, have a disagreeable odor, or have no smell at all. It may be very colorful or have little color. Regardless of color or scent, the flower is important.

Notice the different parts of the flower in the picture. The *sepals* are green and protect the unopened flower. *Sepal* comes from a Greek word meaning ''covering.'' The petals are often brightly colored and have many different shapes and forms. Sometimes there is only one petal and sometimes there are several. The petals attract insects and birds. Why is this important?

Look at the flowers in the photographs. Can you name any of them? Do they have separate petals? Do any have only one petal? The word *petal* comes from a Greek word meaning "leaf." Did you know that a petal is a kind of leaf?

Stamens are the male reproductive part of the flower. They produce millions of tiny, yellow bodies called *pollen grains*. Pollen grains are so small that they look and feel like talcum powder. Sperm cells are produced inside the pollen grains. What other group of plants has pollen grains?

In the center of the flower, and usually surrounded by the stamens, is the *carpel*. The carpel is the female reproductive part of the flower. The bottom part of the carpel is called the *ovary*. The ovary contains one or more ovules. The egg cells are located inside the ovules. After fertilization the ovules will become seeds. The top part of the carpel, the *stigma*, is quite sticky. The middle portion of the carpel is usually slender and is called the *style*.

In order for sexual reproduction to take place in flowering plants, pollen grains from the stamens must land on the top of the carpel. This transfer of pollen is called *pollination*. When pollen is carried from the stamen to the carpel in the same flower it is called *self-pollination*. When pollen is carried from the stamen of one flower to the carpel of a flower on another plant, it is called *cross-pollination*. Peas are self-pollinating plants and most trees are cross-pollinating.

Have you observed a bee on a flower? You know it is collecting food for itself, but did you know it is doing something for the flower as well? Insects, wind, birds, bats, and other mammals act as pollinators. Insect-pollinated flowers are quite showy: they have colorful petals and a sweet smell to attract insects, such as butterflies, bees, and wasps. When bees crawl into flowers looking for nectar, they pick up pollen on their hairy bodies and carry pollen from flower to flower.

Hummingbirds do not have a very good sense of smell, but they have an excellent sense of vision: they are attracted to bright red or yellow flowers. Bats, on the other hand, cannot see very well, but they have a keen sense of smell. They are attracted to sweet-smelling flowers that are dull-colored and open at night. These flowers also produce large amounts of nectar and pollen. The bats, attracted by the scent of the flower, bury their heads into the flower and lap up the nectar with their long, brushlike tongues. They carry pollen from flower to flower on their fur.

Wind-pollinated flowers are not colorful or scented. Why do you think this is so? Grasses and many trees are pollinated by the wind.

Once the pollen grains land on the stigmas of the carpels, a tube begins to grow from each pollen grain. The pollen tubes grow downward through the carpel to the egg cells in the ovary. The sperm cells inside the tubes are then released, and *fertilization* occurs when they unite with the egg cells. While the seeds are being formed, the ovary is undergoing changes and becoming larger. This enlarged ovary is called a *fruit* which forms around the seeds.

When temperature, moisture, and light conditions are right, the tiny plant inside begins to grow, using the stored food. This is called *germination*. Once the germinating plant reaches a certain size, it will make its own food by photosynthesis.

Asexual Reproduction

Asexual reproduction is simply cell division. It does not require two cells (egg and sperm) to come together. Rather, one cell splits into two cells. First, the cell divides its internal parts. Then the two sets of parts pull away from each other until they are totally separate. Finally, the outer membrane of the cell pinches together in the middle, forming two cells from one.

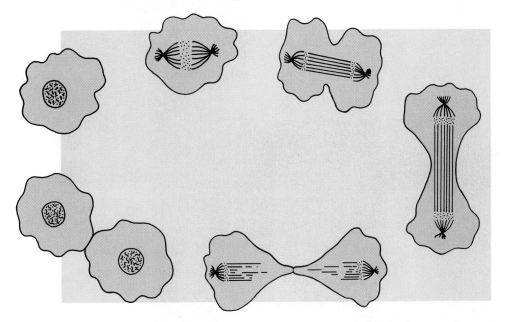

Fragmentation is a very common method of asexual reproduction. A piece, a fragment, of the plant–such as a few cells, stem pieces, or root pieces–grows into a whole new plant. Leaves are another plant part that can grow into a whole new plant. African violet leaves, when placed into moist soil, will grow roots and later stems and leaves. Algae, mosses, liverworts, and fungi have this type of asexual reproduction. *Budding* is common in the yeast fungus. Yeast is a round, single-celled plant. A bulge will protrude from the single cell and finally pinch or "bud" off. The bud then grows into a new plant.

Underground roots and stems are another form of asexual reproduction. Bulbs like onions, runners like strawberry plants, and tubers like potatoes, all can asexually produce new plants.

Man has developed his own methods to produce plants asexually. *Grafting* is usually done with fruit and nut trees. A branch from one tree is joined, or grafted, to another tree that is already growing from seed. The use of *cuttings* is another form of manmade asexual reproduction. Here, a piece of stem with leaves attached is placed into water or wet sand. Roots will form on the bottom of the cutting. The cutting is then transplanted into soil where it will grow into a new plant.

Finding Out . . .

About Fragmentation

1. Get a sweet potato, a carrot with a top, a *Coleus* leaf with stem, an African violet leaf, three clear plastic cups, a shallow dish, toothpicks, some water, some sand, and an X-acto knife.

2. Stick toothpicks around the middle of the potato. Rest the toothpicks on the rim of a glass so that the smaller end of the potato is in the glass. Add water until one third of the potato is covered. Put it in a warm spot and add water as needed. Cut an inch off the top of the carrot, keeping the leaves on. Put the piece of carrot into a shallow dish filled with water.

3. Put the *Coleus* stem into a glass of water. Keep the stem watered and in a shady place. Make three crosswise cuts in the main vein of the violet leaf, and press the leaf into a glass filled with damp sand. Keep the sand warm and moist.

4. Check on your fragmentation experiments over the next two weeks, and record your observations.

Breeding

Scientists can use pollination to produce plants with specific characteristics they desire. Suppose they want to produce a pink morning glory. They would take the red morning glory and the white morning glory and cross-pollinate them. This procedure of pollinating, or breeding, plants includes the science of *genetics*. Genetics is the study of how traits are passed from parent to offspring. The scientists hope that the white and red colors of the parents will blend to make a pink flower in the new plant.

Some characteristics are stronger or more likely to show up than others. In the 1800s Gregor Mendel discovered that when he crossed a tall pea plant with a short one, more often than not, a tall plant was produced. He inferred that tallness was a characteristic more likely to be passed on than shortness. He decided to test his theory.

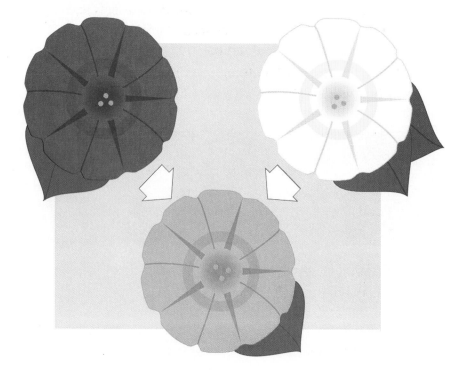

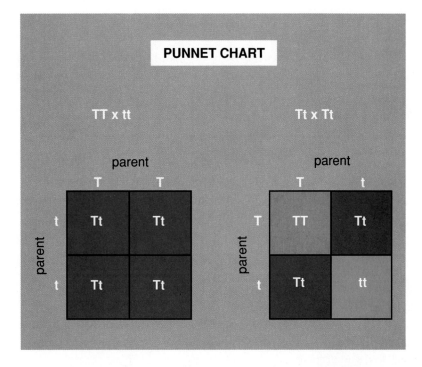

PUNNET CHART

TT x tt

Tt x Tt

Mendel crossed the tall and the short pea plants and got two tall pea plants. He then crossed those two new pea plants and got three tall plants and one short one. He was confused for a while, but after many experiments, he concluded that the tall factor would make the plant tall whenever it was passed down. Only when two short factors came together would the plant be short.

Later scientists made a chart to help clarify Mendel's findings. The capital *T* stands for ''tallness,'' and the small *t* stands for ''shortness.'' When a purely tall plant and a purely short plant are crossed, the tall plant gives the new plant a *T* and the short plant gives it a *t*. Since the *T* is stronger than the *t*, the new plant will be tall.

But the new plant will now have both tall and short factors. When two such plants are crossed, they may produce purely tall plants, purely short plants, or tall plants that have both factors. Look at the chart to see how this happens.

Finding Out . . .

About Genetics

1. Get some red cellophane, some blue cellophane, other colors of cellophane (optional), a pair of scissors, and your notebook.

2. Cut two circles about the size of quarters from each color of cellophane. Place the circles on your notebook chart as directed. Lay the circles over each other. Be sure you never have more than two pieces of cellophane together at one time.

3. You may want to experiment with other colors of cellophane. If you do, try making a combination and have your science partner guess what the "parent" colors are.

 # Animal Reproduction

"And God created great whales, and every living creature that moveth, which the waters brought forth abundantly, after their kind, and every winged fowl after his kind: and God saw that it was good. And God blessed them, saying, Be fruitful, and multiply, and fill the waters in the seas, and let fowl multiply in the earth. And the evening and the morning were the fifth day. And God said, Let the earth bring forth the living creature after his kind, cattle, and creeping thing, and beast of the earth after his kind: and it was so."

Genesis 1:21-24

Some tortoises live more than one hundred years, and some redwood trees live more than a thousand. But all living things, whatever their life spans, grow old and eventually die. Aging and death are consequences of man's fall–part of the curse God put upon the earth. However, God does not allow the earth to become a wasted, barren sphere, hanging silently in space. He has provided ways for life to go on, even though individual organisms die. In the great cycle He has established to keep the earth replenished, birth is as common as death.

The Means of Continuing

Animals must be able to produce others like themselves, or they would all eventually disappear from earth as a species. Most animals reproduce one of two ways–and some can reproduce either way or both ways.

Sexual Reproduction

Because it requires cells from two sexes, this way of reproducing is called sexual. Each male and female produce a sex cell called a *gamete. Gamete* comes from a Latin word for "marriage." Do you think that is an appropriate name? The male sex cell is a *sperm;* the female sex cell is an *ovum.*

When the sperm and ovum join, they form a *zygote. Zygote* comes from a word meaning "to yoke." What does that verb mean? The coming together, the "yoking," of two gametes is *fertilization.*

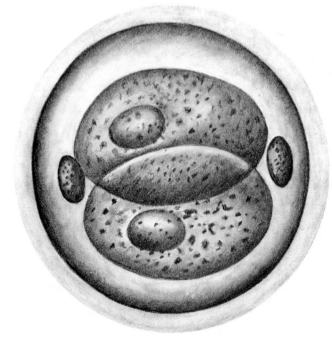

Fertilization can occur in three ways. In some animals it takes place inside the female's body. In other animals it occurs outside the body. For example, the female salmon lays eggs unfertilized in the water. The male salmon then covers them with a milky liquid containing sperm. *Self-fertilization* can happen only in animals that are able to produce both kinds of sex cells–the sperm and the egg cells–in the same organism. Some tapeworms have the ability to reproduce this way.

After fertilization, a zygote grows in one of two places, either inside or outside the mother's body. Most mammals carry their young inside their bodies. A very few mammals–such as the kangaroo and the opossum–carry their young inside their bodies for a brief time. When the young are born, they crawl to pouches on the outside of the mother's body and stay for a longer time, until completely developed.

The opossum bears her young when they are barely half-formed. In fact, about eighteen newborn opossums will fit in a teaspoon. Small as they are, though, they can pull themselves three inches or so to their mother's pouch. Inside the fur-lined pouch they keep warm and well fed for the three months more that they need to develop fully.

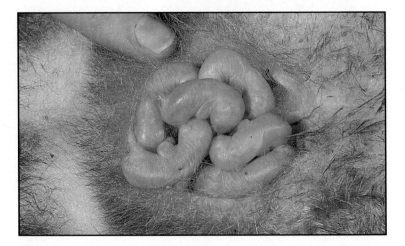

A few mammals, most reptiles, most fish, and all birds lay eggs. The duck-billed platypus and the spiny anteater are two most unusual animals. They are mammals that lay eggs. The platypus lays two, sometimes three, eggs about the size of jellybeans. The eggs stay in a nest of damp leaves deep in a tunnel until they are ready to hatch. The spiny anteater's eggs are a little smaller. Both animals need much care when they hatch out of the eggs.

Most reptiles and fish lay their eggs and then leave, never returning to care for the young that hatch. The young hatch already able to care for themselves. Fish usually lay a great number of eggs. A cod, for example, may lay as many as seven million eggs a year. Why do you think some animals produce so many eggs?

Some fish do care for the eggs they lay. The male sea catfish carries the eggs in his mouth for a month. When the eggs hatch, the fish still carries the young for another two weeks until they are nearly two inches long. Then they are big enough to care for themselves, and the male catfish lets them go. During those six weeks, the father catfish does not eat.

Alligators probably give their offspring more attention than any other reptile. The female alligator makes a mound of plants and mud, pushing the sides up with her legs and strong tail. She then forms a hole in the top of the mound and lays as many as seventy eggs there. Then she covers the eggs with more mud and debris. While the eggs are in the mound, the female alligator guards the nest. When the young alligators are hatching out, they make a grunting sound. The mother alligator paws away the lid she had put on earlier and the little alligators dig their way out. They stay with their mother for almost a year before they venture forth on their own.

Birds do not lay as many eggs as most reptiles and fish. What can you say about the connection between the number of eggs an animal lays and the care it gives them? For the most part, the fewer eggs an animal has, the more care it gives them.

Most birds build nests to house their eggs. God has designed each bird to be able to make its particular kind of nest. Birds come out of the shell knowing how to build their own kinds of nests. Scientists removed some canary eggs from their nest and *incubated* them, kept them warm, until they hatched. When those birds laid eggs, the scientists took those eggs and hatched them artificially. When several generations of canaries had passed without even seeing a nest, the scientists supplied the youngest birds with nest-building materials. The canaries promptly built a canary nest, just as their wild ancestors had. What does this behavior teach us about animal instinct?

When birds have a nest ready, the female begins to lay the eggs. Usually she lays the eggs one at a time, sometimes one a day. She does not incubate them, however, until the last or next-to-last egg is laid. Why do you think that is? Owls are an exception. They will usually incubate the eggs as they are laid. In an owl's nest there may be eggs, newly hatched birds, and fledglings–young birds with feathers–all together. What special problems might owl parents face?

Emperor penguins do not build nests. After the female lays her egg, she goes out to sea. The male holds the egg on top of his feet and covers it with a special flap of loose skin that hangs down from his stomach. The egg stays warm there, even in cold weather. The male penguin never puts the egg down for the two months of incubation. He moves from place to place with an odd, shuffling walk, keeping the egg off the ground at all times. By the time the egg hatches, the female is back, and both parents care for the new bird.

Many birds work in pairs to care for their young. Such cooperation is often necessary, because feeding four or five gaping mouths is hard work. Robins bring food to the nest about a hundred times a day. Wrens often make two hundred trips a day for food. Hawks bring whole rabbits or other prey to the nest and tear off bits for the young, making far fewer visits to the nest.

An egg is a remarkable haven for a young developing animal. God has designed the perfect container for fragile life. Eggs provide protection from the cold, the heat, and the drying action of the wind and sun. They also keep out harmful bacteria and excess water. Furthermore, the eggs allow the life inside to get air, provide it with nutrients, and absorb its waste. Some eggs even change shape and size to accommodate the growth of the occupants.

Eggs that are laid in water usually do not have hard shells. The tiny eggs are encased in a clear, jellylike fluid that protects them well enough in water. Can you think of a reason that the material around the egg should be clear? What if it were red or black or blue? Some eggs contain a drop or two of oil which makes them float. Other eggs, mostly freshwater eggs, are sticky. Picking up grains of sand soon after they are laid, the eggs become heavier. What do you think happens to these eggs? They sink. Why should eggs in rivers or streams sink rather than float?

Eggs on land almost always have hard or leathery, tough shells. Such eggs, when they contain a growing life, have several compartments, or *sacs*. The yolk will provide nourishment for the animal as long as it is in the shell. On this yolk is a tiny circle called a *blastodisc,* where the zygote will develop into an *embryo*. An embryo is an organism in its early stages.

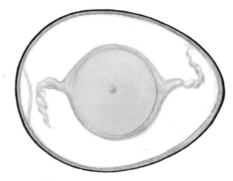

The yolk and the blastodisc are surrounded by a thin membrane, a sac. When the yolk sac is still inside the shell, it is connected to the inner lining of the shell by two twisting bands of tissue called *chalazas*. What do you think the chalazas do?

Another sac contains the *albumen,* a fluid that contains nutrients and provides the animal with a safe, comfortable kind of water bed. *Albumen* comes from a word that means "white." Why is the fluid around the yolk called albumen? Can you think of another word that comes from the same root that refers to an animal that has white hair and red eyes?

Another sac collects waste products from the growing animal. A fourth sac just inside the shell holds the other three sacs snugly together. This tissue has a network of blood vessels that carry air to and from the little animal through minute pores in the shell. Even inside a shell a new life must breathe. What would happen if a shelled egg were underwater too long? The life inside would suffocate.

The shell is an efficient packaging material. It protects the forming animal from bumps and blows. Sometimes its mottling or coloring provides camouflage, protecting it from predators. The shell contains calcium, which makes it strong. As the animal grows, the calcium is absorbed into the animal's bones. How will this transfer of calcium prove beneficial when hatching time arrives? The shell will be softer and the animal will be larger and stronger than when the egg was first laid. Both changes will make hatching easier.

Many eggs, mostly bird eggs, are camouflaged. The shells are colored and marked to help them blend in with the environment. Reptile eggs are plain white. They do not need colors or specks for protection because their mothers usually bury them in the ground or under stones or leaves.

Eggs are not always "egg-shaped." Turtle eggs, for example, are round. The eggs of the murre, a sea bird that often lives on ledges, are lopsided. What advantage is there for the murre in having uneven eggs? They will not roll easily and therefore will not fall from the ledges as often as smoother eggs would.

In a few snakes, and a rare turtle or lizard, the eggs hatch *inside* the mother's body. The young are actually born alive, but they developed in shells like other snakes.

Finding Out . . .

About Eggs

1. Get a chicken egg, a magnifying glass, and a plain saucer.

2. Look at the unbroken egg under the magnifying glass. Describe how it looks. Can you see any pores?

3. Break the egg carefully into the saucer, being careful not to tear the yolk. Let the egg stand a few seconds.

4. Using the magnifying glass, study the egg. Can you see the blastodisc? Can you identify the other parts?

Why do you think that mammals are not usually hatched from eggs? Mammals are better protected inside their mothers' bodies than they would be inside an egg. And they can take a longer time to develop. This method is also more practical in most cases. Think what an enormous egg it would take to store enough yolk to nourish a baby whale!

How long do you think mammals would have to incubate the eggs? It takes fifteen days for a baby hamster to grow big enough to be born, nine weeks for puppies to grow enough, five months for sheep, about nine months for a cow, and twenty-two months (nearly two years!) for a baby elephant. What problems would such lengthy incubations cause for the mammal parents?

After birth, mammals need care from their parents, some more than others. Baby rabbits grow enough to care for themselves in just a few weeks. A rabbit may raise as many as three families in one summer. Baby foxes are usually born in April, and by September they are grown enough to care for themselves. Elephants sometimes stay with their mothers until they are twenty-two years old.

Some people interpret the care that mother animals give their young as loving attention. Animals behave out of instinct, not emotion. For example, the relationship between mother sheep and lambs is a matter of timing and availability rather than love. A female sheep will accept any lamb as her own for a few hours after she has given birth. But after about three hours, the sheep will reject any lamb, including her own, if it has been away from her. The first few hours after birth seem to be a period of *imprinting,* or establishing a bond between mother and offspring.

Young animals learn how to survive by watching the adults. They learn what to eat, how to find food, where to hide, and when to sleep. They often practice these skills in their play. Lion cubs sometimes mock in their rough-and-tumble games the techniques they will later use to bring down prey and kill it.

The age at which animals are grown up enough to produce their own offspring varies greatly. Mice are ready at six weeks, rabbits at four or five months, chimpanzees at eight years, and elephants at twelve years. Why do you think such animals as mice and rabbits need to reproduce so much more rapidly than chimps and elephants?

Finding Out . . .

About Hatching

1. Get one dozen or so ladybug eggs from a science supply company. Or collect several live ladybugs in early spring and keep them in a net-covered jar with fresh plants and aphids for them to eat. Perhaps you can find some ladybug larvae.

2. Keep the ladybugs, eggs, or larvae in a covered jar with plants and aphids. Watch the jar for several days.

3. What do ladybug eggs look like? Do the young ladybugs look like their parents? What do they eat? Record your observations. Then let the ladybugs go.

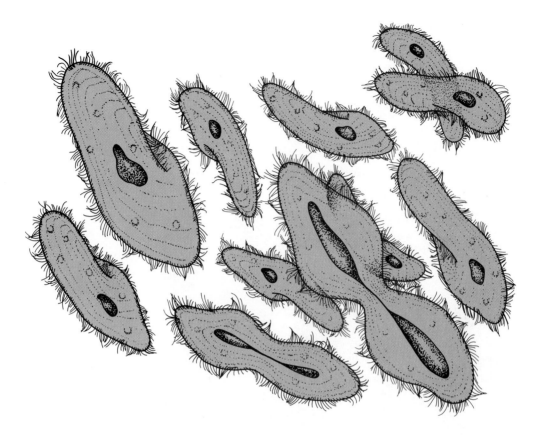

Asexual Reproduction

Some animals can reproduce without the joining of gametes. The smallest animals undergo *binary fission*. *Fission* comes from a word meaning ''split,'' and *binary* comes from words meaning ''two by two.'' One-celled animals can split into two equal cells; and those two cells can each split in two–and so on.

The paramecium is a tiny water animal that reproduces itself by splitting in two. It is shaped something like a microscopic football with many hairs or projections all around that help it move through the water. When it reproduces, the paramecium gets narrower and narrower in the middle. Then it looks something like an hourglass. Finally, the narrow place in the middle seals off and separates, and two paramecia exist where before there was only one.

Other animals can reproduce through *fragmentation.* The animal breaks up (or is broken up) into parts or fragments. Each part then develops into a completely new animal. For example, a starfish has five rays, or arms. If the arms are cut off, each will grow into a new starfish. Starfish can, however, also reproduce sexually, by external fertilization. Why do you think some animals, especially the smaller ones, have more than one way of reproducing?

The planaria is an organism that lives in water. It travels along the bottom of ponds, searching for food. If anything should cut off its tail, the planaria grows a new one. If the animal gets cut in half (either sideways or lengthwise), two whole planarians usually develop. Planarians also reproduce sexually by forming small cocoons.

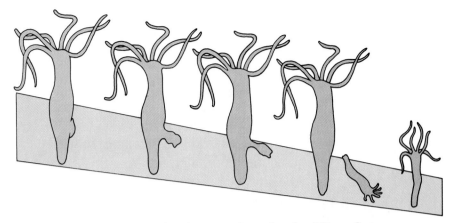

Still other animals reproduce by *budding*. Sometimes a group of cells will enlarge in an organism, becoming an outgrowth. Eventually, the outgrowth, or bud, separates from the parent and becomes a new individual. Sponges often reproduce this way.

Animals that have been sexually reproduced have characteristics from both parents. They are not exactly like either parent. How do you think asexually reproduced animals are different from sexually reproduced ones?

Finding Out . . .

About Fragmentation

1. Get some planarians from a biological supply company or from a pond, distilled water, culture dishes, a dissecting knife, a pipette or a thin straw, and a boiled egg.

2. Prepare a jar of distilled water (or spring water). If you capture your own planarians, use the water they were found in.

3. According to your teacher's instructions, cut a planaria in half. Put the pieces in separate culture dishes of water. Put the dishes in a cool, dim area and cover. Keep the planarians for two weeks or so. Do not feed them during their regrowth.

4. If you want to keep the planarians after they have regrown, you must change the water daily. Carefully remove the planarians with a pipette first. Every day drop in a crumb of the egg yolk. Do not overfeed (50 planarians need only a pea-sized portion). When the planarians have eaten, remove the egg remains with a pipette.

5. Keep a record of changes you observe in the planarians.

 **Tracks**

When you see an animal, you can identify it by its size, shape, color, and behavior. But there are many animals afoot that you may never see. They may come out only at night, or they may stay in the woods, or they may be so small you do not notice them. But you can still find out about their behavior and even identify them. How?

Everything that moves about on land usually leaves prints. A rhinoceros does; a mouse does; you do; cars do; even tumbleweeds do sometimes. Tracks can be found everywhere–in snow, in sand, in soil, in dust, in thick carpets. With a little experience and a little patience, you can become a track investigator. You do not need any special equipment, and you do not need to go on a safari.

Size of Prints

One of the first things a tracker looks at is the size of the prints. Usually the bigger the print, the bigger the animal. You have probably seen more cat and dog tracks than any other kind. Look at the cat and dog prints below. Which animal do you think made each track? One was made by a 190-pound mountain lion; one was made by a twenty-pound coyote; one was made by a six-pound house cat.

When you study a track, it helps to have a measuring tape and a sketchbook. Always measure the print at the longest place. Include the toenail marks in the length. Measure the print at the widest part as well. Then write down the dimensions or draw the print in your book, recording the measurements. Be sure that you never step on the tracks you are studying.

A big dog will have a bigger track than a small dog will. But a dog will almost always have a slightly bigger track than a cat the same size. What do you think the largest dog is? What is the largest cat? The cat in this case has a bigger print than the dog.

The tiger is a large cat; the wolf is a large dog. A wolf can weigh up to 150 pounds. How much do you think a tiger weighs? The adult male tiger weighs about 420 pounds.

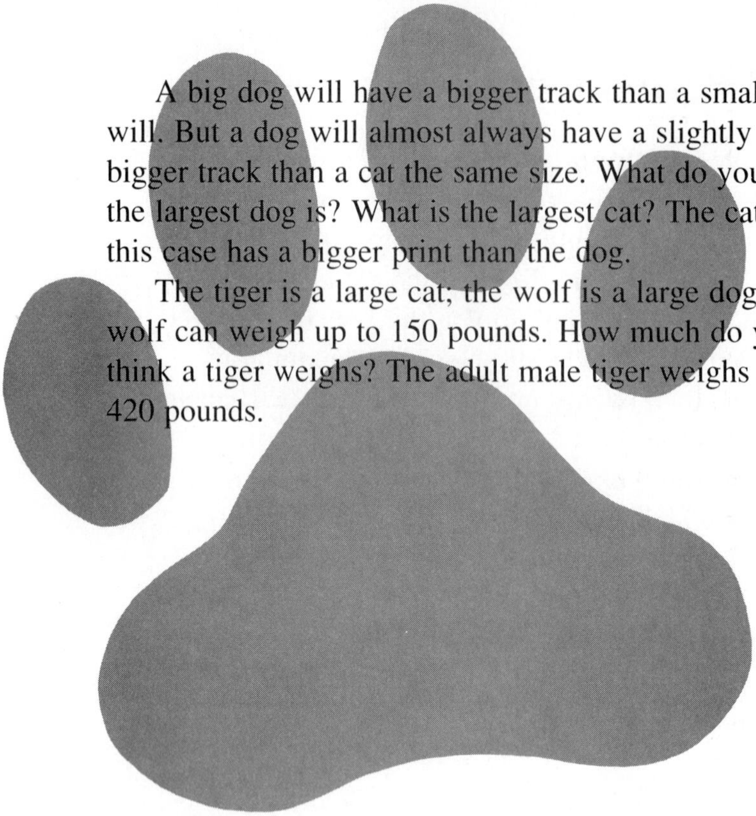

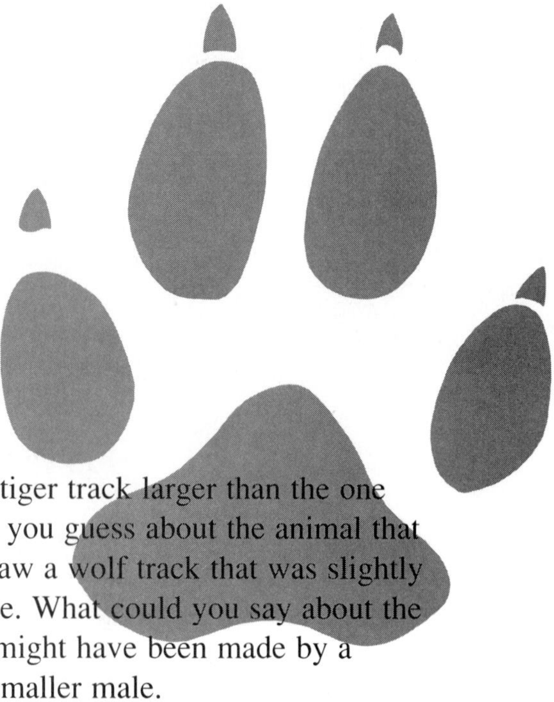

If you came upon a tiger track larger than the one shown here, what could you guess about the animal that made it? Suppose you saw a wolf track that was slightly smaller than the example. What could you say about the animal that made it? It might have been made by a female or by a lighter, smaller male.

Some animals have relatively small feet for the size of their bodies. Whitetail deer, for instance, have rather dainty feet. A male whitetail usually weighs about 180 pounds but can weigh nearly 250. Its hoof is neatly tapered and split. The print of a whitetail is about the size shown here. Does it surprise you that an animal that large has so trim a foot?

The whitetail's foot has *dewclaws*–small, hard stubs just above the hoof on the back of the leg. Sometimes the dewclaws also make a print in the soil or snow. Can you think what would cause the dewclaws to become part of the track a deer makes? When a deer steps in soft earth or in fairly deep snow or when it is running hard, the dewclaws give it extra support.

Shape of Prints

Look at the cat and dog tracks on this page. How are cat tracks different from dog tracks? Cat tracks never show claw prints. When it is walking, a cat pulls its claws up. Dogs' nails cannot be retracted; so they sometimes show up in tracks. Also a cat's foot pads make a little more rounded print. What do you notice about the size of the toe prints in the cat and dog tracks? The cat has smaller toes compared to its heel pad than a dog does.

Animals with hooves make other kinds of tracks. Horses have unsplit hooves. Cows have split hooves. So do deer. How would you tell a cow track from an elk track? Both tracks would be about the same size. One way to tell would be by the shape. A cow track is generally more nearly round than an elk print, being shaped something like two large kidney beans turned inward. The elk print is more pointed.

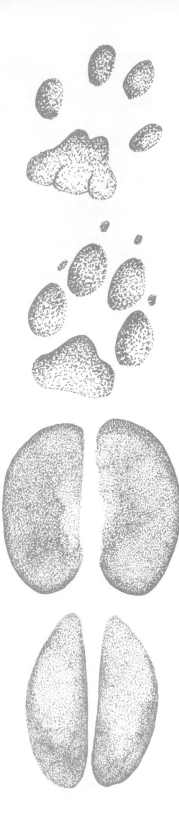

Finding Out . . .

About Prints

1. Get some plaster of Paris, water, paper cups or paper plates with sides about one inch high, a spoon, paper towels, and a pet animal. If you do not have a pet, your own bare foot will do.

2. If you are using your pet's foot, have the animal ready. If the animal's foot is small, use a paper bowl lined with plastic wrap. For a large animal foot or your own foot, use a paper plate. Make a fairly thick mixture of plaster of Paris, and pour it quickly into the container. Let the mixture settle for about ten minutes. Then press the animal's foot or your foot firmly into it.

3. Pull the foot up slowly and gently. Wipe the plaster off the foot immediately. Let the plaster in the cup or plate harden. Study the print. What can you tell from the print? What can you not tell?

Pattern of Prints

Sometimes the individual prints are not distinct enough to identify the animal that made them. But you can still make several observations. The pattern of the prints can tell you, for one thing, whether the animal was hopping, walking, or running.

Animals that hop, like rabbits, push up and forward from their back feet. The back feet land beyond the front feet, making a track that has four footprints in a rough *V* or *Y*. The front feet usually are placed one in front of the other. In deep snow the front feet often land together.

You can also tell something about where the animal lives. Rabbits are hoppers that live on the ground. Other hoppers live mostly in trees. Squirrels, for instance, live in trees and hop when they are on the ground. Their hind feet come forward past the front ones when they move. But their front feet usually stay together.

Look at the tracks on this page. Were they made by a rabbit or a squirrel? How do you know? Can you think of other animals that hop? What kind of tracks do you think they make?

Birds also leave tracks that tell how they move and where they spend most of their lives. Birds that spend a lot of time on the ground usually walk, putting one foot in front of the other. Tree-dwelling birds usually hop when they are on the ground. Look at the tracks on this page. Where do the birds probably live that made them? Not all birds only walk or hop. Robins do both. What do you think a robin's track might look like?

God designed each animal with its own special track and its own way of getting around. Because tracks are different for every moving thing, people are able—after observing and recording tracks—to identify them and even make predictions from what the tracks tell.

When you know general shapes and patterns of tracks, you can also sometimes tell from indistinct tracks which direction the animal was going. Look at the tracks here. Which way was the squirrel going?

When an animal runs, it makes a different pattern of tracks from when it walks or trots. A cat, for instance, makes a single line of tracks when it walks. When it runs, it makes another pattern. Which picture shows where a cat was running? A walking dog makes pairs of tracks. Its back foot comes forward and makes a print slightly forward of the front foot on the same side. When a dog runs, he moves his feet differently, making a different pattern of tracks. How different do the tracks of a running dog look from those of a running cat?

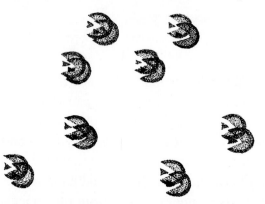

Walking or trotting horses make pairs of hoof prints. Can you say how they walk? Their hind feet fall near the prints made by their front feet. How do you think you might be able to tell whether a horse was walking or trotting? If it was trotting, the pairs of prints would be somewhat farther apart.

Can you tell from the arrangement of tracks what animal was here? Can you say how it was moving? Can you say which way it was going?

ASCIENCE IN ACTION Wildlife Photography

One profession that makes use of tracking skills is wildlife photography. The beautiful pictures of elk and elephants and eagles that appear in books and magazines are the results of long hours of watching, tracking, and waiting.

Most wildlife photographers hike and camp to get near their subjects. They keep detailed notebooks, recording such information as where deer are bedded or the direction of a lion track. One photographer, by following tracks and signs of rubbing and browsing, came upon two whitetail bucks preparing to spar. He was able to get his camera ready without being noticed, and his patient tracking was rewarded with splendid pictures of the antlered clash.

Sometimes wildlife photographers go after much smaller game, following lizards across sandy flats or trailing a lemming over the tundra. Whatever they are after, the photographers must be aware of animal habits and habitats. Some photographers rewrite their notes into books, which they illustrate with their own photographs.

What other science skills do you think a wildlife photographer uses?

Finding Out . . .

About Casting Prints

1. Get some plaster of Paris, a jar of water, a spoon or stick to stir with, some paper cups, several strips of stiff paper, a paper clip, a table knife, and a field guide to tracks.

2. Go outside. Choose a day after a rain, or walk along a lake or stream. Look for animal tracks in firm mud. Never step on tracks you find. Walk beside them. When you find a print that is clear and easy to get to, try to identify it. Then, make a cast of it.

3. Make a collar that is just a little larger than the print with the paper strip and the paper clip. Put the collar in the ground around the print. Mix some plaster of Paris in a paper cup. Be sure to get the plaster just the right thickness. Plaster too thin will be crumbly when it dries; plaster too thick will not yield a good cast. Stir in enough water to make a mixture about the consistency of pancake batter. The mixture should flow smoothly and slowly.

4. Pour the plaster into the print carefully. Cover the print completely. It is not necessary to fill the collar, but a thick cast will last better. Wait about twenty minutes. The plaster will get warm as it begins to harden. When the plaster starts to cool, loosen the dirt around it with a table knife. Lift the cast and let it harden completely.

5. Wash any dirt off the cast. What can you tell about the animal that made the track? How is the cast easier to study than the actual print? How is it more difficult?

Common Tracks

Have you ever seen any of these tracks? What can you say about the animals that made them?

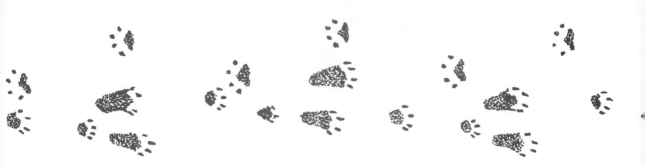

Reading the Signs

Look at the picture here. Were the animals going the same direction? How do you know? What animals made the tracks? Do you think the animals passed by at different times? Why do you think so?

The rabbit was heading to the right. The cat was going left. The animals probably came by at different times, because neither animal changed course or speed. Would a rabbit keep hopping along slowly that close to a cat? How does knowing animals' habits help you read their tracks?

INSIDE Information

Expert trackers learn many of their techniques by watching how animals hide from and find each other. One outdoorsman studied mice for weeks to learn how to know an owl was near when he could not see it. He discovered that mice are alert to many clues he had overlooked, such as the speed and pattern of a shadow passing overhead. Another naturalist learned to find a certain beetle by watching the lizards that eat them.

It is important to note where the track is. Is it under pine trees? Is it in a field? Is it by a pond or a lake? Since some tracks look very much alike–a dog's and a fox's, for example–where they are found can often give you a clue to identifying them.

Sometimes there are other signs that can help you. Occasionally animals pass by rough bark or brambles, leaving bits of hair or fur. Sometimes only a few hairs rub off. Where do you think you would be most likely to find hairs? Often animals chew or rub against trees and bushes. Rabbits, for instance, gnaw off small saplings and twigs on a slant. Their bites leave clean, smooth edges. Deer chew off shrubs down to about two feet high. Where they have chewed is ripped and ragged. The male deer rub the velvet off their horns on trees, leaving torn bark and bits of the soft antler covering behind. Bears turn over logs and rocks, rip open stumps, and chew on trees four or five feet up from the ground.

It also helps to be able to tell how long ago the track was made. The clearer the track, the newer it probably is. Prints in snow usually do not last long. Neither do tracks in sand; wind or water soon erase them. What can you say about a track that has grass growing in it?

Look at the tracks on this page. Can you tell what happened?

Look at the photographs here. Can you guess what made each track?

Even the most experienced tracker will sometimes find a trail he can only guess at. Animals do not always walk and behave according to the field guides. But by staying alert to signs around you, you can often tell what went on just before you arrived.

Finding Out . . .

About Reading Tracks

1. Get three or four pounds of flour, cornstarch, or some other odorless powder, some bread, cut fruit, seeds, and a field guide to tracks. (If there happens to be soft mud, sand, or a light new snow in your area, you will not need the flour, cornstarch, or powder.)

2. Choose a time when there is no rain expected. Find a dry, even place outside where few people come by. Put the food in the middle of the area. Dust the flour (or other material) evenly all around. Smooth the flour with the edge of a sheet of paper if you like. Leave the area until the next day.

3. Check the area the next morning and afternoon. When you see the food has been disturbed, try to read the tracks to find out how many animals have been around, what kind of animals they are, and which way they went.

4. Record your findings. Sketch the area and make detailed drawings of the tracks.

About Stories Tracks Tell

1. Get a white sheet of paper, an ink pad, a piece of raw potato, a pocket knife, a field guide to tracks, and a pen.

2. Choose an animal or animals whose hind feet are nearly the same as the front feet, such as a horse or a cat. Draw the print of one foot on the potato. Then carve the potato down, leaving the print raised. Repeat for each animal.

3. Make a track picture using the potato as a stamp. Press the potato onto the ink pad often so that the prints stay clear. Be sure to get the pattern of prints correct.

4. Trade your picture with someone else in the class. Can you read the story in the tracks?

"Doth not he see my ways, and count all my steps?"
                                        Job 31:4

Glossary

acid rain rainwater that has more acid than normal

anemometer *(an•ə•mom′ i•tər)* instrument used to gauge wind speed

angle of attack the angle of an airplane wing to the wind

atmospheric pressure the weight of the air on the earth

atomic theory of matter a way of understanding matter by assuming it is made up of tiny parts called *atoms*

atom the smallest part of an element that can join other elements

baleen *(bə•lēn′)* strips of whalebone that hang from the roof of some whales' mouths for straining food from seawater

barometer *(bə•rom′ i•tər)* instrument for measuring atmospheric pressure

bathyscaphe *(bath′ i•skaf)* deep-diving craft

binary fission *(bī′ nə•rē fish′ ən)* division of a cell that produces two cells

brain stem the part of the brain that leads to the spinal cord and controls involuntary functions

cast sediment impression of a mold

cerebellum *(ser•ə•bel′ əm)* the part of the brain that coordinates voluntary movement

cerebrum *(ser′ ə•brəm)* the largest part of the brain, including the frontal, parietal, occipital, and temporal lobes

chimney a spring under the sea that spews out minerals

chromosphere *(krō′ mə•sfîr)* a transparent layer of gas around the photosphere

cirrus *(sîr′ əs)* high, transparent, wispy clouds

condensation process by which a gas becomes a liquid

conduction the passing of heat through one thing to another

continental shelf a gently sloping rock platform from the beach to the continental slope

continental slope a steep drop at the end of the continental shelf

convection the movement of heat by fluid motion

Coriolis effect *(kôr•ē•ō'lis)* tendency of the earth's rotation to turn the direction of a moving object or fluid to the right in the Northern Hemisphere and to the left in the Southern Hemisphere

corona *(kə•rō'nə)* the bright, irregular ring of hot gas above the sun's chromosphere

cumulus *(kyo͞om'yə•ləs)* low, white clouds that appear fluffy and mounded

current a stream of steadily moving water within a larger body of water

desalinization *(dē•sal•ə•ni•zā'shun)* process of removing salt from water

diameter the thickness or width of something

drag the force that holds an airplane back

element any matter that is made of only one kind of atom

energy the ability to do work

fertilization the joining of ovum and sperm

flare a sudden explosion of energy on the sun

fossil parts of living things and marks made by living things that are preserved by nature

front area of contact between two air masses

gamete *(gam'ēt)* a sex cell

gas a state of matter having no definite shape or volume

genetics *(jə•net'iks)* the study of how characteristics are passed from generation to generation

gravity the force that tends to draw two objects together

gray matter the special nerve tissue of the brain and spinal cord

Hadley cell a cycle of rising and falling air near the equator

heat energy associated with the movement of atoms and molecules

hurricane intense storm with high winds swirling around an eye

imprint mold of an extremely thin organism

imprinting process by which some young animals learn behavior by watching a role model

lift the force used to overcome gravity

light year the distance light travels in a year

liquid a state of matter that has a volume but no definite shape

mass the measure of the amount of matter in a body

matter anything that takes up space and has mass

Milky Way the galaxy in which our solar system moves

mold hollow outline of an organism in rock

molecule the smallest part of an element that can still have the characteristics of that element

neuron *(noor′on)* a sensitive cell in the body, a nerve cell

Newton's third law of motion law that says that for every action there is an equal and opposite reaction

nucleus the center of some atom models

ocean basin floor of the sea

oceanography *(ō•shə•nog′rə•fē)* the study of the sea

ozone layer protective band of special oxygen around the earth

paleontology *(pā•lē•on•tol′ə•jē)* the study of ancient living things

paleozoologist one who studies fossils of animals with backbones

photosphere *(fō′tə•sfîr)* the surface of the sun

plankton tiny plant and animal life in the sea

pollen powdery material of flowering plants containing sperm

precipitation particles of ice or water that fall from the atmosphere and may reach the ground

radiation the passing of heat through open space

reflex an involuntary action or response

relative humidity the amount of water in the air compared to the amount that could be there

reproduction the process by which organisms produce more of the same kind

seed the part of the plant that forms after fertilization

solar eclipse an event that happens when the moon blocks the sun's surface from earth's view

solid a state of matter that has a definite shape and volume

sperm male sex cell

spinal cord strands of nerves leading from the brain stem down the backbone

stratosphere *(strat′ ə•sfĭr)* the layer of the atmosphere above the troposphere

stratus *(strā′təs)* clouds in a dense layer over most of the sky

sunspot a dark area on the sun that is probably an area of magnetic activity

thermometer instrument for measuring temperature

thrust the force that makes an airplane go forward

tornado small, intense wind storm

troposphere *(trō′pə•sfĭr)* the layer of atmosphere in which we live

tsunami *(tsōo•nä′mē)* tidal wave

vertebrate animal with a backbone

volume the measure of the amount of space a three-dimensional object takes up

Index

Photo Credits

Cover: Marty Snyderman (large), NASA (top inset), Unusual Films (bottom inset)

Title Page: Marty Snyderman

Suzanne R. Altizer: 11, 41 (large), 59, 62 (left), 78, 97, 101, 112, 130, 136, 148, 150, 162, 164, 167, 168, 175, 178 (both), 183 (inset), 196, 201 (large), 202 (top right, bottom right), 205 (right), 217 (top right, bottom left)

Aruba Tourist Bureau: 161

Teresa Barnett: 202 (left)

Brad Carper: 61, 131 (large)

George R. Collins: 9, 19, 21 (large), 45, 54, 62 (right), 73 (inset), 80, 81, 87, 89 (right), 90, 91, 96 (top), 139, 144, 147 (inset), 172 (right), 184, 190 (top), 199, 205 (right), 220

Terry M. Davenport: 41 (inset), 44, 58, 153, 156-7, 172 (left)

Timothy N. Davis: 96 (bottom left)

Department of Energy: 95 (large), 131 (inset)

Eastman Chemicals Division of Eastman Kodak Co.: 111, 145

Kenneth Frederick: 165 (both), 166 (all), 174 (all), 215

Bruce Iverson: 32

Breck P. Kent: 1 (both), 5 (both), 57 (large), 170 (both), 183 (large), 186, 187, 190 (bottom), 192, 195, 198, 214, 217

Library of Congress: 75, 84 (top)

NASA: 22, 113 (both), 126

NOAA: 67 (both), 68

National Archives: 71

National Optical Astronomy Observatories: 128

National Park Service: 176
  M. Woodbridge Williams: 21 (inset)

Naval Photographic Center: 25

Kathy Pflug: 141

Wade K. Ramsey: 211

Smithsonian Institution: 13 (both)

Marty Snyderman: 37, 38 (both)

Swearingen Aviation Corporation: 92

3M: 147 (large)

U.S. Air Force: 73 (large), 86, 89 (large)

Unusual Films: 7, 8, 28, 29, 40, 43, 47, 50, 53, 56 (both), 63, 66, 69, 72, 79, 82, 93, 100, 103, 104 (both), 105, 108, 129, 134, 137, 140, 142, 143, 146, 155, 160, 169, 179, 183, 188, 193, 200, 207, 218, 219

Ward's Natural Science Establishment, Inc: 6, 57 (inset), 96 (bottom right)

Dawn L. Watkins: 201 (inset), 217 (bottom right)